INTERSPIRITUAL
MEDITATION

InterSpiritual Meditation

A Seven-Step Process from the
World's Spiritual Traditions

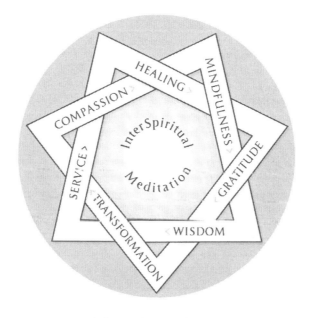

Workbook and Journal

EDWARD W. BASTIAN, PH.D.

Spiritual Paths Publishing

SANTA BARBARA, CALIFORNIA

2013

Spiritual Paths Publishing

6 Harbor Way, Santa Barbara, CA 93109
www.spiritualpaths.net

Spiritual Styles Mandala™ is a registered Trade Mark (™ 2013) of Edward W. Bastian, Ph.D.

Edited and formatted for publication by Zachary Malone.

Cover design by Lynda Rae, Aurora Design Studio.

Back cover photo credit: Michael Stinson.

Manufactured in the United States of America.

ISBN: 978-1-4802-5794-8

InterSpiritual Meditation

ISM is a contemplative process that can be shared by people from diverse perspectives and traditions. It can be practiced alone and in community with others. It pulls together key elements of contemplation and meditation shared by many traditions. In this process we gather in the language of silence and experience inter-connectedness. Joining in stillness, we don't impose on others our own personal beliefs, rituals, or the names for our absolute truths, deities or God. We honor and celebrate the wise and compassionate practices of all traditions. We discover a profound unity within our diversity. We flourish in the love, peace, compassion, gratitude and the strength of our shared wisdom. We are of one heart. Quietly, each in our own way, we join in the following seven stages together. The sound of a bell leads us from one stage to the next.

This workbook and Journal is designed to be used for guided personal study, contemplative mentoring, retreats and workshops (in person & online) in conjunction with two books:

InterSpiritual Meditation:
A Seven-Step Process from the World's Spiritual Traditions

Meditations for InterSpiritual Wisdom:
Practices and Readings Drawn from the World's Great Spiritual Traditions.

http://www.spiritualpaths.net/spiritual-paths-books

For more information on the Spiritual Paths Institute,

Spiritual Paths seminars, and courses in InterSpiritual Meditation, please

visit www.spiritualpaths.net, www.interspiritualmeditation.org,

or email ed@spiritualpaths.net.

Table of Contents

InterSpiritual
Meditation

OVERVIEW

Preface

During the past forty-five years, my inner life has been profoundly shaped by wonderful teachers, colleagues and students, along with life's many challenges. Because of my deep gratitude to this process, I want to share a meditative practice that emerged from my personal transformation. I hope it will inform and benefit your personal practice as well as your interactions with people from the world's marvelous variety of contemplative traditions and belief systems.

My commitment to Buddhist formation practice began in my mid-twenties and when I began learning Tibetan and Sanskrit and studying with extraordinary teachers in monastic settings in both South Asia and America. The fruits of this training ripened in wonderful ways during over the past ten years as I worked closely with over forty Christian, Buddhist, Muslim, Jewish, Hindu, and Buddhist, Taoist, and Native American teachers in our Spiritual Paths programs and books.

InterSpiritual Meditation is the result of both my hope for a mature personal contemplative practice, as well as my hope to formulate a universal practice that can be done engaged in harmony with people of many traditions. Actualizing both hopes have has been profoundly informed by my collaboration with great meditative practitioners with a variety of spiritual and secular methods.

Firstly, from the perspective of a personal meditation practice, I have learned that each meditator must take personal responsibility for the method and the outcome of his or her practice., In my case, a practice which is at the same time Buddhist and while also inclusive of other traditions became my authentic mode. While our teachers and colleagues can impart their wisdom and experience, the actual practice of meditation is something we have to engage alone, though with their continued blessings. Working alone, with occasional guidance from our teachers and mentors, we must learn to cultivate the internal processes of our minds, accentuating the positive and eliminating the negative. This work is invisible to the outside world. It is subtle and refined. Like many of life's most precious skills, mindfulness and quiescence of mind takes years to cultivate. Meditation is both profound art and subtle science. It is a cultivated taste. Therefore, in the kitchen or laboratory of our minds, we must personally apply the science, the recipes, insights, methods, skills, patience and perseverance we have learned from others.

Secondly, through many sessions of group meditation with teachers of diverse practices, I have experienced the presence of shared consciousness even though we are all doing different internal practices. In spite of, or perhaps because of our diverse practices, I have found that we actually co-create an inter-spiritual consciousness that is greater than the sum of its parts. It is this shared experience that I believe can be a foundation for peace among peoples of all spiritual and non-spiritual beliefs. In this experience we know for certain that we can no longer look at each other as the "other." We become inextricably and tangibly linked to such a degree that to harm another is to harm our self.

During the past few years I have taught many courses and completed two books on InterSpiritual Meditation. However, I realized that I needed to do something more to help people engage in this practice. Therefore, I have compiled this workbook and journal. This journal is a work in progress meant to be used along side the books, the classes, courses, individual mentoring and workshops. I hope it will help you develop and refine your own meditative practice, and to work in contemplative alliance with others whose inspiration and practices emerge from the world's marvelous variety of beliefs, practices and traditions.

Introduction

The world's religions have developed many types of contemplation and meditation, each formulated for specific spiritual purposes and specific types of practitioners. InterSpiritual Meditation is neither a replacement nor a synthesis of these. Rather it provides a process drawn from many traditions that can help individuals develop a practice that is at once personal and inclusive. Therefore it also lends itself for use by groups of people from diverse traditions and with diverse individual practices. The following verse by Rumi helps illustrate this possibility:

> If ten lamps are present in one place,
> each differs in form from another;
> yet you can't distinguish whose radiance is whose
> when you focus on the light.
> In the field of spirit there is no division;
> no individuals exist.
> Sweet is the oneness of the Friend with His friends.
> Catch hold of spirit.
> Help this headstrong self disintegrate;
> that beneath it you may discover unity,
> like a buried treasure.
> (*Mathnawi I, 678-83* of Jalaluddin Rumi,
> translated by Camille and Kabir Helminski in *Rumi Daylight*)

Because InterSpiritual Meditation is a vibrant and dynamic process and not a one-size-fits-all conclusion, it might provide you with a foundation for a life-long contemplative practice. Life-long, because (a) each step in the process leads us into deeper and deeper realms of discovery and realization, and (b) our own practice evolves and deepens over the course of our lives. Taken together, all the so-called steps are mutually interdependent and provide a context for spiritual maturation.

This workbook and journal are designed to support both in-person and online seminars and workshops in conjunction with two of our other books, "InterSpiritual Meditation: A Seven-Step Process from the World's Spiritual Traditions," and "Meditations for InterSpiritual Wisdom: Practices and Readings from the World's Spiritual Traditions."

This workbook can also be used in conjunction with my other book and course of study called "Creating Your Personal Path." This work is designed to help us to honor our Archetypal Spiritual Styles, Discern Answers to our Spiritual Questions, and cultivate practices that are compatible with our spiritual predispositions.

Following are the primary goals for this workbook:

o   To explore the emerging paradigm of InterSpirituality.

o   To discover the processes of contemplation and meditation shared by the world's spiritual traditions.

o   To identify and honor a contemplative focus that matches your primary spiritual styles.

o   To develop and refine both a personal and group meditation practice that is sustainable, satisfying, and inclusive.

o To gain the knowledge, skills, and experience required to facilitate InterSpiritual Meditation sessions with individuals and groups. (A subsequent certificate program will help you learn to lead InterSpiritual group sessions.)

The organization of this workbook presupposes your commitment for ongoing study, discussion, journaling, contemplation, meditation and application in everyday life. Its contents include the following:

o An introduction to familiarize you with the general purposes and goals.

o Definitions of key terms and concepts relating to InterSpirituality.

o An overview of the entire seven-step process of InterSpiritual Meditation.

o Individual sections containing poems and scriptural quotes, as well as questions for each of the seven steps to help your develop and refine your own practice.

o Guidelines for InterSpiritual group discussions.

Through this workbook I will provide you with a process to engage in the inner art and science of meditation in a way that is compatible with your own life experience, spiritual perspectives, spiritual learning style, questions, chosen tradition, and the teachings and examples of others. This process will help you recognize, cultivate and utilize the special capacities of consciousness that can be your internal allies for transformation. It will also aid you in bringing together practices and perspectives you have gained in your previous studies with other teachers and traditions. In this way, these seven steps will provide a container in which you can include accumulated wisdom from may sources.

Your journaling will help to marry your intellectual understanding and your contemplative and meditative experience into a single, coherent and comprehensive practice. Based on the extensive writings in your journal, you will create brief summaries of your personal purpose, content and focus for each of the seven steps of contemplation and meditation. Each step in your meditation will be based on the summaries of your journal writings.

This workbook contains poems, stanzas and scriptural passages from many spiritual traditions that pertain to each of the seven steps. These will help inspire and stimulate your own contemplative process to be recorded in the journal. If you have your own favorite poems, writings, and songs to further stimulate your journaling, please liberally incorporate these as well.

This workbook will be posing many questions intended to stimulate and further inspire your search for personally meaningful answers. These questions are designed to help you dig deeply, to gain clarity, to open up to the contemplative wisdom of other great teachers and to bring forth your inner knowledge. You need not be confined by the questions listed here. Rather, honor your own spontaneously arising questions and trust that this contemplative process will help you find answers.

Through a process of systematic journaling and meditation on each of the seven steps, you will forge and refine a meditation that is at once rooted in your tradition, while also a reflection of the sum total of your life experiences and experiments with truth.

Please remember that steps 1–4 are contemplative. Here, as you focus on each topic, you will bring to mind your personal journal summaries for each. These summaries provide the content for your contemplation.

In steps 5–6 you enter into the actual meditation. Here, you engage your mind in a more single pointed, non-conceptual focus on your chosen objects of meditation. This can be the meditation you already practice or one that you create for this particular process. If you don't have a specific meditation practice, the breathing meditations explained in the two books will provide you with a place to begin. Your journaling will also help you to refine the objects and purposes for these steps of meditation.

Finally, in Step 7, you return to the contemplative mode as you formulate the dedication you have developed in your journaling.

The combination of meditation and journaling will deepen and strengthen your capacity to be transformed into your ideal being with the qualities you most want to embody. With each step, your mind will be carefully nurtured and prepared for the next steps. In the end, all the steps are mutually interdependent, helping to support and sustain each other.

Defining Key Terms

Please become familiar with the following terms and the ways they are defined in the context of our work. We will be discussing these in class, in our online forums and personal mentoring sessions. Please reflect on these terms and definitions in your journal.

InterSpirituality

"Humanity stands at a crossroads between horror and hope. In choosing hope, we must seed a new consciousness, a radically fresh approach to life drawing its inspiration from perennial spiritual and moral insights, intuition and experience. We call this new awareness interspiritual, implying not the homogenization of religion, but the recovering of the shared mystic heart beating in the center of the world's deepest spiritual traditions."
- Brother Wayne Teasdale, *The Mystic Heart*

Religion

"Religion I take to be concerned with faith in the claims to salvation of one faith tradition or another, an aspect of which is acceptance of some form of metaphysical or supernatural reality, including perhaps an idea of heaven or nirvana. Connected with this are religious teachings or dogma, ritual, prayer and so on."
- His Holiness, the Dalai Lama, *Ethics for the New Millennium*

Spirituality

"Spirituality I take to be concerned with those qualities of the human spirit—such as love and compassion, patience, tolerance, forgiveness, contentment, a sense of responsibility, a sense of harmony—which bring happiness to both self and others."
- His Holiness, the Dalai Lama *Ethics for the New Millennium*

Spirituality pertains to the essence, or the spirit of our very existence. It entails an intuitive wisdom and experiential knowledge --- *gnosis, sophia, prajna, hokhmah, da'at, hikmah* --- that transcends our senses and intellect. It is the natural instinct that draws us to the conscious essence at the core of our being. It is the innate impulse that connects us to a higher power, that which we may relate to as a universal essence, a divine entity, the primordial state of being or the Ultimate Reality. It is the instinctive impulse for wisdom and compassion, to be loving and altruistic. Spirituality gives an ultimate meaning and purpose to human life through which we can evolve to our greatest potential.

Interfaith

The terms "interfaith" and "interreligious" pertain to the impulse to find shared values, principles and customs among the world's religions and to work together with tolerance and respect for the common good.

Interfaith programs bring together people of various religions to share their beliefs, ethics, customs, principles, rituals, rites of passage and holidays. These programs generally focus on the social values and cultural forms of different religions and avoid metaphysical and institutional differences that lead to conflict.

InterSpiritual

The term "InterSpiritual" pertains to the contemplative, meditative and mystical experiences that are the foundation for spiritual practice.

InterSpirituality connotes an inclusive state of contemplative consciousness that merges with those spiritual experiences that were the creative force for the major religions. It holds the promise of a genuine *sharing* of our respective spiritual experiences and a conscious joining at the deepest levels of our being. InterSpirituality represents the next phase of understanding and connectivity between people of different spiritual traditions.

Contemplation

Contemplation may be characterized by deep concentration, as well as profound inner observation, insight, analysis and non-conceptual intuition, all involving and yet surpassing the intellect. It is a profoundly reflective state of consciousness that can arise, for example, while sitting in silence, reading, being in nature or even while engaging in the appreciation of art or music. Spiritual contemplation can be a quality of consciousness that rests within porous boundaries between non-conceptual meditative absorption and subsequent conceptualization of transcendent experience. Contemplation is our means of consciously traveling back and forth between the sacred and the profane, the divine and the worldly, the mystical and our ordinary reality.

Meditation

Meditation is a technique for attuning consciousness, which, depending on the individual, the technique used, and the spiritual context in which it is done, may lead to altered states of awareness (including profound focus and tranquility), states that are measurably beneficial and transformative for individuals and groups.

In this specific usage, meditation is an activity that enables human consciousness to fulfill its potential to be tranquil, one-pointed, blissful, non-conceptual, wise, compassionate, intuitive and unified with the truth of our existence. This truth, and the name by which it is termed, may vary depending on each tradition and each individual.

Prayer

Prayer is a powerful spiritual and psychological tool for setting our purpose and intention, for focusing our energy on an intended result. Whether prayer is directed to a divine being, a higher power, within our self, or into the universe, we are evoking a deep personal wish that is far more profound than the mundane desires that generally run through our minds. Prayer activates the capacity of our consciousness to actualize or manifest our most profound and benevolent aspirations for ourselves and others.

InterSpiritual Meditation

InterSpiritual Meditation is a universal process drawn from the world's spiritual traditions. It helps individuals to cultivate inner peace, wisdom and compassion. Its seven-step process enables people of different spiritual practices to create engaged contemplative communities based on empathy, understanding, shared contemplative intentions and compassionate service for the common good. Each of the seven steps provide containers within which meditators can include the wisdom and methods from one tradition, a variety of traditions and from their own personal life experience.

Spiritual Genome

Just as each biological species has its own unique genome that gives it life and vitality, so are the founders' spiritual experiences to the life and vitality of each religious tradition. The job of the contemplative is to re-experience this original spiritual original genome in order to breathe life and vitality into each tradition. Without this, traditions die and fossilize. Just so, human spirituality must be revitalized by direct experience.

Spiritual Diversity

Just as biological diversity is required for the health of each individual within each species, so is spiritual diversity required for the spiritual health of the planet. Just as species must rub up against each other to reinvigorate the life forces required for survival, so must religions come into contact to stimulate each to regenerate their essential life force.

Biological and Spiritual Diversity

InterSpiritual Meditation is not a genetic hybrid. It is not a new religion. It is a process wherein meditators from each tradition can help each other revitalize the unique spiritual genes required both for spiritual diversity and personal spiritual realization. The vitality, viability and relevance of all religions, spiritual traditions and people depend, directly or indirectly, on interaction with each other. Indeed, the survival on the human species may depend on this interdependent interaction with the deepest levels of our inter-being-ness.

Open-Source Spirituality

The term "open-source" comes from the language of computer programmers who share code with each other from various sources to enhance their respective programs or operating systems. This implies an openness to share and to benefit from the wisdom gained by others. Yet it also presupposes that each programmer has learned basic skills of a specific programming language as a foundation on which to build and to include the insights of others. Just so, InterSpiritual Meditation builds on the wisdom and processes of many diverse contemplative traditions. As with computer programmers, InterSpiritual meditators will benefit from a grounding in a single contemplative tradition as a foundation for open-source spiritual inquiry, sharing and adaptation.

InterSpiritual Meditation

A SEVEN-STEP PROCESS

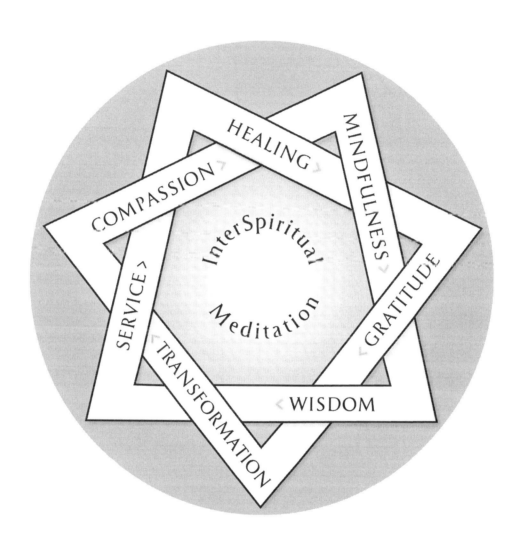

AN INTEGRATED PROCESS FOR
PERSONAL & GROUP PRACTICE

InterSpiritual Meditation – Seven-Step Chart

	MENTAL STATE	PRAYER	ATTRIBUTES
1	Motivation	May I Be Healthy and Happy	Mind Body Spirit
2	Appreciation	May I Be Grateful	Remembrance Thankfulness Trust and faith Devotion Prayer Offering Sacrifice
3	Transformation	May I Become My Highest Ideal	Imagine the Ideal Self-Assessment Confession Remorse Forgiveness Inward Love & Compassion Surrender Commitment
4	Intention	May I Be Loving and Compassionate	Sympathy & Empathy Exchange self and others Interdependence Universal Reciprocity Universal Essence
5	Attention	May I Be Mindful Through Breathing	Body Position Focus on Breath Patience Observation & Vigilance Perseverance Recollection Concentration
6	Meditation	May I Become Wise Through Meditation	Tranquil Focus Insight *Via Positiva* and *Via Negativa* Bliss Equanimity Unity
7	Dedication	May I Be In Service to All Beings	Bring this meditation into all relationships and situations in the coming days.

A Brief Description

This contemplative process can be shared by people from many perspectives and traditions. It can be practiced alone and in community with others. It pulls together key elements of contemplation and meditation shared by many traditions. In this process we gather in the language of silence and experience inter-connectedness. Joining in stillness, we don't impose on others our own personal beliefs, rituals, or the names for our absolute truths, deities, or God. We honor and celebrate the wise and compassionate practices of all traditions. We discover a profound unity within our diversity. We flourish in the love, peace, compassion, gratitude, and the strength of our shared wisdom. We are of one heart. Quietly, each in our own way, we join in the following seven stages together. The sound of a bell leads us from one stage to the next.

1. Motivation: May I Become Healthy in Mind, Body, and Spirit

Physical, mental, and spiritual health are intertwined, and meditation fosters their good health and happiness. We begin meditating with confidence and determination that it will help us heal the innermost causes of illness and suffering. We pray that InterSpiritual consciousness will help heal all beings.

2. Gratitude: May I Be Grateful for Life's Many Gifts

With gratitude we invoke and honor our teachers, mentors, and great spiritual role models. We invite these great beings to remain present and pray that they guide us. We remind ourselves about the blessings of friends, family, and the environment that nurtures and sustains us.

3. Transformation: May I Be Awakened and Transformed Into My Highest Potential

We acknowledge and confess our shortcomings, vowing to patiently persevere in our personal transformation. We vow to remove our inner obstacles and negativities. Without guilt, we forgive others and ourselves as we open to the transformative presence of love.

4. Intention: May I Be Loving and Compassionate

We set our intention on love and compassion -- the transforming energy for the health and happiness of all. We vow to help all beings be free from the causes of their suffering.

5. Mindfulness: May I Be Centered and Mindful Through Breathing

Mindfully, we concentrate on our breathing. This calms, clears, and focuses our mind. Thoughts, memories, and feelings are observed and released. We focus on our breath, drawing it into the heart-center of our being. Opening ourselves to the reciprocity of universal love, healing, and wisdom we establish the tranquil focus for deep meditation.

6. Meditation: May I Become Wise Through Meditation

Meditation and contemplation are taught in many ways by many traditions. With sincere respect and appreciation for others and dedication to our own practice, we silently engage in our own meditation. Alone or in community we deepen of our own wisdom as well as our InterSpiritual communion with other diverse experiences of that which we call "sacred."

7. Dedication: May I Bring Love, Compassion, and Wisdom Into the World

Visualizing our family, friends, colleagues, antagonists, and all beings throughout the world we rededicate ourselves to becoming servants of peace, justice, and environmental health. May this meditation help us to engage together in the world with patient kindness and wise compassion.

STEP ONE

MOTIVATION

"MAY I BE HEALTHY AND HAPPY"

We hate misery, but love its causes.
We love happiness, but refuse to cultivate its causes.

\- Buddhist law of reversed effect, Alan Watts

STEP 1: MOTIVATION

"May I be Healthy and Happy"[i]

It is not easy to sustain a regular practice of meditation. Therefore we need a strong motivation. For some, the personal goal of health and happiness may seem selfish and not worthy of a compassionate contemplative practice. Whether we admit it or not, however, our own health and happiness is an unavoidable goal. Achieving it, as we will see, entails a profound process of transformation that is entailed in the six steps that follow. So, our prayer for health and happiness is a practical and honest place for most of us to begin. Looking after our own health and happiness can provide the motivational starting place we need to sustain a regular practice of contemplation and meditation.

Even the neurological and medical sciences are proving the value of a regular practice:

> Meditation has been shown to reduce both the experience of chronic pain and its inhibition of everyday activities. Pain-related drug utilization was decreased and activity levels and self-esteem increased.
> - Kabat-Zinn 1982, 1985, 1987

> Not only do studies show that meditation is boosting their immune system, but brain scans suggest that it may be rewiring their brains to reduce stress... Ten million American adults now say they practice some form of meditation regularly.
> Stein, J. (2003) *The Science of Meditation*, TIME magazine (cover story), August 4: 48-56.

Poems, Stanzas and Scriptural Passages

Below are inspirational verses from various traditions to help stimulate your own contemplation and journaling for Step One.

"The Law of Reversed Effect"

We hate misery, but love its causes.
We love happiness, but refuse to cultivate its causes.
- Alan Watts

"Four Worldly Dharmas"

Gain and Loss: When we seek things to make us happy, we are often frustrated in the attempt, angry when they don't, or saddened by their loss; therefore, we suffer.

Pleasure and Pain: When we seek happiness through sensual pleasure, our longing and attachment to the pleasure, or sadness from the pain of unfulfilled expectations inevitably leads to pain and suffering.

Praise and Scorn: When we seek happiness through the praise of others, this praise eventually leads to scorn and jealousy, which are the result of the ignorance that gave rise to the desire in the first place.

---

[i] For additional information on Step One, please refer to the book *InterSpiritual Meditation*. The following verses, poems, and quotes are provided to stimulate your journaling.

[ii] For additional information on this step, please refer to the book *InterSpiritual Meditation*. The following materials are

Fame and Ill Repute: When we seek happiness through fame, the examination of our most minute flaws becomes the occupation of others, and we are eventually held in ill repute because of them.

Hinduism

Instill in us a wholesome, happy mind
With goodwill and understanding.
Then shall we ever delight in your friendship
Like cows who gladly rejoice in meadows green.
This is my joyful message.
- *Rig Veda* X, 25:1

Buddhism

May I be well.
May I be happy.
May I enjoy good health.
May I be peaceful.
May all my good purposes by fulfilled.

May all sentient beings everywhere,
In all realms, in all world systems, be well.
May they be happy.
May they enjoy good health.
May they be peaceful.
May all their good purposes be fulfilled.

- *Visuddhimagga* 9: 9-39
Quoted by Bikkhu Bodhi in *Meditations for InterSpiritual Wisdom*

Taoism

Health is the greatest possession.
Contentment is the greatest treasure.
Confidence is the greatest friend.
Non-being is the greatest joy.
- Unknown

Judaism & Christianity

Happy is the one who finds wisdom
And gains understanding.
- *Proverbs* 3:13

Questions to Stimulate Contemplation and Journaling

The following questions are posed to stimulate your journaling. Please add you own questions or rephrase these so they have greater personal meaning. Your journal writings will help you formulate your own personal contemplative focus for this step.

What is your definition for health and happiness?

Can constant, sustainable health and happiness come solely through external causes?

What changes in your inner life are required to be healthy and happy?

What is the relationship between a healthy mind, body and spirit? How are they mutually dependent?

Do health and happiness require you to be loving and compassionate? Why or why not?

Do health and happiness require you to change your attitude and values? If so, what changes would be necessary?

Do health and happiness require you to change your diet and exercise, life habits, such as your career? If so, are there other poignant changes you foresee?

Do health and happiness require you to change the quality of my mind and consciousness? If so, what changes might be required?

Do you need deep and abiding purpose and meaning for your life in order to be healthy and happy?

What is the purpose of contemplation and meditation in accomplishing these objectives?

Your Contemplative Practice

Please remember that the purpose of the above quotes and questions are to stimulate your exploration through writing in your journals. Through your journaling practice, please explore your own deepest personal conclusions as well as your beliefs that have been molded by your tradition, teachers, mentors or role models. You might also do additional research on the internet, in books and conversations with other teachers and students. Then, reflecting on your writings, create a brief summary that will be the contemplative focus for this step.

As you begin, say to yourself with conviction: "May I be Healthy and Happy." This will serve not only as a prayer, but also your self-directed challenge to discover and activate the true inner causes of health and happiness. With this determination, engage in meditation to cultivate these causes and to eliminate the obstacles to health and happiness. In your contemplation, bring to mind the summary of your journal writings and vow to actualize these in your life.

By beginning this contemplation with a prayer, we open ourselves to the transformative power and support of the vast and untapped potential of consciousness and our greatest potential.

STEP TWO

APPRECIATION

"MAY I BE GRATEFUL"

I enter the Silence.
I listen to the great guardians,
Trees, without whose breath we cannot live.
I offer prayers of gratitude to the plants and nature,
For it is through nature that we are guided to the Infinite.
Nature is the good spirit that guides us
And shows us how to live in harmony and balance.

- Tezkalci Matorral Cachora, Yoeme/Lacandon Maya

STEP 2: APPRECIATION

"May I be Grateful"[ii]

Each day of our lives we have a choice whether we approach life with pessimism and resentment or optimism and gratitude. The perspective of gratitude does not require us to be Pollyannaish or romantic, rather it enables us to welcome the opportunities and blessings that flow from every pleasant, neutral or unpleasant situation, person and moment of our life.

Poems, Stanzas and Scriptural Passages

Below are inspirational verses from various traditions to help inspire your own contemplation and journaling for Step Two.

Lacandon Maya

Before Grandfather Sun comes up,
I arise to offer sacred smoke
And prayers to the Maker and Shaper.
I send my prayers on the wind, to the four directions.
I ask Creator to take pity on humanity
For we are seeking our correct path.

I enter the Silence.
I listen to the great guardians,
Trees, without whose breath we cannot live.
I offer prayers of gratitude to the plants and nature,
For it is through nature that we are guided to the Infinite.
Nature is the good spirit that guides us
And shows us how to live in harmony and balance.

- Tezkalci Matorral Cachora, Yoeme/Lacandon Maya

Native American

O Great Spirit, whose voice I hear in the wind and whose breath gives life to all the world, hear me. I come before you, one of your many children. I am weak and small. I need your strength and wisdom. Let me walk in beauty and make my eyes ever behold the red and purple sunset; my ears sharp so I may hear your voice. Make me wise, so I may learn the things you have taught my people; the lessons you have hidden under every rock and leaf. I seek strength not to be superior to others, but to come to you with clean hands and straight eyes, so whenever life fades, like the fading sunset, my spirit will come to you without shame.

- Chief Yellow Lark Blackfoot

[ii] For additional information on this step, please refer to the book *InterSpiritual Meditation*. The following materials are provided to stimulate your journaling.

Judaism

It is good to give thanks unto the Lord,
To sing praises unto Your Name, Most High,
To proclaim Your loving-kindness in the morning,
And Your faithfulness every night.
- Psalms 92: 1-2

Our Family Prayer (Universal)

We give thanks for our variety of skills and interests;
For our different ways of thinking, moving and speaking;
For common hardships and common hopes;
For this family gathered here;
For living together and eating together;
For all our good times, and not so good times;
For growing up and growing older;
For wisdom deepened by experience;
For rest and leisure;
For the privilege of work;
For time made precious by its passing;
For all that has been,
And all that will be;
For all these blessings, we give thanks.

- Bastian/Winslow/Irons Family Prayer from unknown source

A Simple Prayer

Thank you *God* for all that grows,
Thank you for the sky's rainbows,
Thank you for the stars that shine,
Thank you for these friends of mine,
Thank you for the moon and sun,
Thank you *God* for all you've done!
- Source Unknown

Buddhism

You, Universally Honored.
Are a great benefactor.
By doing this rare thing,
You have taught and benefited us
Out of your compassion toward us;
I will never be able to repay your favors,
Even if I try for millions of kalpas;
I will never be able to repay your favors,
Even if I bow respectfully to you,
Offering my hands or feet and everything else;
I will never be able to repay your favors,
Even if I carry you on my head or shoulders

And respect you from the bottom of my heart
For as many kalpas as there is sand in the River Ganges.
- *The Lotus Sutra, verse 4*

Secular

Gratitude unlocks the fullness of life. It turns what we have into enough, and more. It turns denial into acceptance, chaos to order, confusion to clarity. It can turn a meal into a feast, a house into a home, a stranger into a friend. Gratitude makes sense of our past, brings peace for today, and creates a vision for tomorrow.

- Melody Beattie

- - - - - -

We clasp the hands of those that go before us,
And the hands of those who come after us.
We enter the little circle of each other's arms
And the larger circle of lovers,
Whose hands are joined in a dance,
And the larger circle of all creatures,
Passing in and out of life,
Who move also in a dance,
To a music so subtle and vast that no ear hears it
Except in fragments

- Wendell Berry

Praying
It doesn't have to be
the blue iris, it could be
weeds in a vacant lot, or a few
small stones; just
pay attention, then patch
a few words together and don't try
to make them elaborate, this isn't
a contest but the doorway
into thanks, and a silence in which
another voice may speak.

Mary Oliver

Questions to Stimulate Contemplation and Journaling

When we examine the teachings of the world's contemplative traditions we begin to see concurrence regarding specific mental attributes to be cultivated in the practice of gratitude. Here, I have listed seven of these as a foundation for your journaling and contemplation. These are remembrance, thankfulness, trust and faith, devotion, prayer, offering and sacrifice.

For each of the mental attributes I have included a series of questions to stimulate your journaling. Your journal writings will help you formulate your own personal contemplation focus for this step.

Remembrance

In this step of our meditation, we remember with profound gratitude some of the people and ideals that help us to develop sustainable health, happiness, purpose and meaning.

Who and/or what are those people and/or principles that truly help you to develop deep and sustainable health and happiness?

What are the positive aspects in your life and your relationships for which you can be grateful?

What are the elements of nature, the earth and the universe that give you life, sustaining and enlivening you?

What are challenges in your life that can help you to deepen your wisdom, patience, compassion and life perspective?

Who are the teachers, exemplars and role models, either contemporary or historic, whose teachings have enriched your life and giving it meaning?

What are the teachings, the principles, the truths and the perspectives that give reason, meaning and purpose to your life?

Thankfulness

A completely sincere and explicit attitude of thanks refines our internal mental environment. It creates the mental foundation wherein the objects of our gratitude can be internalized, embodied or integrated. Therefore, having first remembered those beings and things that help us to achieve sustainable health, happiness, wisdom, compassion and spiritual direction, we now give sincere thanks to them from depths of our mind and heart.

Trust and Faith

To endure and overcome the obstacles we need abiding faith that the goal will be worth the effort. Now, having remembered and given thanks to those that help us to live a happy and healthy life with meaning and purpose, we generate and renew our trust and faith that these will help fulfill our goals.

Devotion

In order to achieve our personal goals and ideals, we must be very devoted to them. Devotion is a profound and practical mental quality that fuels the commitment, perseverance, patience and energy we need to actualize our highest ideals. At this stage, we bring forth a deep and sincere devotion to actualize and sustain those ideals and practices in which we have placed our trust and faith.

Prayer

The word "prayer" connotes the most sincere and fervent wish that a human being can make. It signifies our humble openness to receive the blessings from that which we consider the source of divine wisdom, love and ultimate fulfillment. Whether prayer is directed to another being, to the depths of our own consciousness, to God or to a universal power, we are evoking a deep personal wish that is far more profound than the mundane desires that generally occupy our minds. Prayer activates the potential of our essential being to actualize our most profound and benevolent aspirations for both our self and others. The efficacy of prayer can be measured in our sense of peace, in our steadfast determination to achieve even the most difficult tasks and our capacity to help comfort and heal others.

Offering

A material, mental or virtual offering is a powerful way to seal and prove our commitment and devotion to our highest ideal. It is a powerful psychological intention to actualize the teachings of those to whom we are grateful.

What are you willing to offer in order to live you life in alignment with the teachings and ideals of those to whom you are grateful?

What are you willing to offer to achieve your highest life goals?

Sacrifice

Living our life in alignment with these requires giving up, relinquishing or even sacrificing the things in life we are most attached to.

What are you willing to sacrifice to manifest the ideals of those to whom you are grateful?

What are you willing to sacrifice to manifest your most profound ideals?

Your Contemplative Practice

Please remember that the purpose of the above quotes, questions and attributes of gratitude is to stimulate your contemplative writing in your journals. In your writing, please explore your own deepest personal insights as well as your beliefs that have been molded by your tradition, teachers, mentors, or role models. You might also do additional research on the internet, in books and conversations with other teachers and students. Then, reflecting on your writings, create a brief summary that will be the contemplative focus for this step.

As you begin this step, say to yourself with total conviction: "May I be Grateful." This is not only a prayer, but also your self-directed challenge to fully appreciate both the easy and difficult gifts of life for which we can be grateful. With this determination, engage in meditation to cultivate gratitude and to eliminate the negative states of mind that lead to pessimism, depression, antipathy, and self-doubt. In your contemplation, bring to mind the summary of your journal writings and vow to actualize these in your life.

Here, in answer to our prayer, we open ourselves to the transformative power and support of the vast and untapped potential of consciousness and our greatest potential.

STEP THREE

TRANSFORMATION

"MAY I BE TRANSFORMED"

Just as a goldsmith,
Taking an object of gold,
Fashions it afresh into another
New and more beautiful form,
So the atman, discarding this body
And dispersing its ignorance,
Makes for itself another
New and more beautiful form:
That of the Fathers, the spirits, the Gods,
Prajapati, Brahman, or of other beings.

- Brhadaranyaka Upanishad, IV

STEP THREE: TRANSFORMATION –
"May I be Transformed into My Ideal Being"[iii]

In order to make positive changes in our lives, it is very helpful to visualize our ideal life goals, to assess our present condition, to confess our shortcomings, to feel remorse, to forgive and commit to a fresh start. Please contemplate the following questions and formulate your transformative commitments in your journal. Your contemplative writing will provide the foundation for your personal contemplation on transformation, the third step in our meditation.

Poems, Stanzas and Scriptural Passages

Below are inspirational verses from various traditions to help stimulate your own contemplation and journaling on transformation.

Hinduism

Just as a caterpillar,
Having reached the end of a blade of grass
And approaching another one, collects itself
[For making the transition],
Even so this atman, having discarded
The body and overcome ignorance,
Approaching another one
Collects itself [for making the transition].

Just as a goldsmith,
Taking an object of gold,
Fashions it afresh into another
New and more beautiful form,
So the atman, discarding this body
And dispersing its ignorance,
Makes for itself another
New and more beautiful form:
That of the Fathers, the spirits, the Gods,
Prajapati, Brahman, or of other beings.

This atman is in truth Brahman,
Consisting of consciousness,
Desire and desirelessness,
Righteousness and unrighteousness.
According to one's deeds,
According to one's behavior,
So one becomes.

The one who does good becomes good,
The one who does evil becomes evil.
One becomes virtuous by virtuous action
And evil by evil action.
But others say that
The human being consists of desire;
As is the desire, so is the intention,
And as is the intention, so is the action.
And whatever the action, that is what is obtained.

- Brhadaranyaka Upanishad, IV

---

iii For additional information on this step, please refer to the book *InterSpiritual Meditation.* The following materials are provided to stimulate your journaling.

Christianity

Come to know the One
In the presence before you
And everything hidden from you will be revealed....
When you are able
to make two become one,
the inside like the outside,
and the outside like the inside
the higher like the lower,
so that a man is no longer male,
and a woman, female,
but male and female become a single whole...
Then you shall enter in.
- *Gospel of Thomas*, Logion 22

Taoist Precepts

~Becoming One with the Tao~

1. Practice inaction and effortless flow;
2. Be supple and soft;
3. Guard the feminine, and don't be first;
4. Be nameless;
5. Practice purity and tranquility;
6. Engage in only good and skillful behavior;
7. Practice desirelessness;
8. Be contented;
9. Yield and withdraw.

Sufism

Steadfast keep thy strength of heart,
For desires not to divert thy heart.
Concentrate thy powers and might,
For this is the meaning of life.
Purify thy heart in Truth,
Thy mirror is then cleansed and pure.
Thyself unite, for the call Divine,
To reveal in thee all life.

When the heart is pure and clear,
To heaven its journey's then.
When God unfolds thy heart,
Mirror of heart reflects thy lord.
Selfless and pure when life be thine,
Salek of religion as Mohammad doth Shine.
United with God thy life is blessed,
In solitude of heart thou findest faith.

- Hazrat Shah Maghsoud Sadegh Angha, *The Epic of Existence*

"It is just like what happens when all the kernels,
The husks of which have not yet been washed away,
Are disdained by someone who is impoverished,
And said to be something to be discarded.
But although the outside seems like something useless,
The inside is genuine and not to be destroyed.
After the husks are removed,
It becomes food fit for a king.
I see that all kinds of beings
Have a *buddhagarbha (Buddha Nature)* hidden by *klesas*.
I preach the removal of those things
To enable them to attain universal wisdom.
Just as I have a *Tathagata* nature,
So do all beings.
When they develop it and purify it,
They quickly attain the highest path.
- *The Tathagatagarbha Sutra*

Questions to Stimulate Contemplation and Journaling

When we examine the teachings of the world's contemplative traditions we begin to see concurrence regarding specific mental attributes to be cultivated in the process of transformation. I have included over thirty of these in the seven steps of InterSpiritual Meditation.

Here in Step Three, I have included eight of these mental attributes to help you accelerate the process of self-transformation. These are: imagining the ideal, self-assessment, confession, remorse, forgiveness, inward love and compassion, surrender and commitment. Each of these is defined in "InterSpiritual Meditation." To help you contemplate these, I have included a series of questions pertaining to each.

The following questions are posed to stimulate your journaling about each of these mental attributes to be cultivated. Your journal writings will help you to explore and to cultivate these mental attributes as the foundation for your personal contemplative process.

Imagine the Ideal

Who is the person that you most admire and whose qualities you would like to emulate?

What are the qualities of being that you most want to manifest in your life?

What contribution to the world would you most like to make?

What is your deepest purpose for life?

What way of life and inner being would give your life ultimate meaning?

Self-Assessment

From the depths of your heart, what do you most want to become or to manifest in your life?

Who or what are the role models for you to emulate?

What must you learn and who can teach you?

What internal changes are required to accomplish this?

What external life changes are required to accomplish this?

What qualities do you need to cultivate for this transformation?

What obstacles or negativities do you need to overcome or eliminate?

Confession

What is your present condition with respect to your transformative goals?

What things are you doing, thinking, and saying that are not in line with your ideal?

What specific examples of these non-conforming thoughts, words and actions can you bring to mind just now?

Why are these not consistent with your ideal way of being?

Remorse

How do you feel regarding your thoughts, words and actions that do not measure up to your higher standards?

Are you making excuses, or rejecting remorse for fear of poor self-image or esteem?

Are you confusing debilitating, unhealthy self-judgment with objective observation of your behaviors needed to reach your goals?

Forgiveness and Inward Love

Are you able to forgive yourself and not hang on to debilitating guilt?

Are you able to forgive others who might be related or complicit in your unsatisfactory thoughts, words and actions?

Are you able to love and care for yourself just as you would another personal for whom you have unconditional love?

Are you able to forgive yourself without weakening your resolve for transformation?

Surrender

Are you able to surrender to the higher calling of your transformation?

Is this surrender just giving up or acquiescence, or is it giving into your higher calling?

How can surrender become an engaged and proactive intention rather than a passive and non-committed capitulation?

Commitment

Are you fully committed to transformation?

Are you willing to do what it takes to make the changes you desire?

What are the internal obstacles that weaken your resolve?

What are the temptations that lure you away from your goals?

Why do these temptations seem to be superior that your ideals?

Why are these higher ideals superior to your old mental, verbal, and behavior habits?

Your Contemplative Practice

Please remember that the purpose of the above quotes and questions is to stimulate your writing in your journals. In your writing, please explore your own deepest personal insights as well as your beliefs that have been molded by your tradition, teachers, mentors, or role models. You might also do additional research on the internet, in books and conversations with other teachers and students. Then, reflecting on your writings, create a brief summary that will be the contemplative focus for this step.

As you begin, say to yourself with conviction: "May I be Transformed." This will serve not only a prayer, but also your self-directed challenge to achieve your highest potential, to become your ideal being, and to actualize the qualities you most admire. With this determination, engage in meditation to become transformed and to eliminate the negative states of mind that prevent your transformation.

Depending on your way of looking at it, transformation might entail removing the coverings of your natural purity, or eliminating obstacles preventing you from fulfilling your highest potential, or gradually accumulating qualities that you revere. However you look at transformation, the process inevitably entails a combination of emptying out and filling up. We empty out our false sense of self, our negative emotions, and our ignorance. And we fill up with the such positive and virtuous qualifies as love, compassion, wisdom, and unity with that we call the sacred or divine.

In your contemplation, bring to mind the summary of your journal writings on transformation, and vow to actualize these in your life. Here, in answer to your prayer, open yourself to the transformative power and support of the vast and untapped potential of consciousness and our greatest potential.

STEP FOUR

INTENTION

"MAY I BE LOVING
AND COMPASSIONATE"

Love is patient, love is kind;
It does not envy, it does not boast,
It is not proud, nor is it rude;
It is not self-seeking, nor easily angered,
It keeps no record of wrongs.
Love does not delight in evil,
But rejoices in the truth.
Love bears all things, believes all things,
Hopes all things, and endures all things.
Love never ends.

- St. Paul in his *First Letter to the Corinthians*

STEP 4: INTENTION

"May I be Loving and Compassionate"[iv]

The intention of love and compassion are at the heart of all great spiritual and contemplative traditions. They are the foundation for the health and happiness for our self and others. They are the divine intentions for truly spiritual contemplative practice. Since there are times when love and compassion don't spontaneously flow from our hearts, contemplative journaling and practice can help us engender them. The verses and questions that follow are meant to inspire and stimulate your journaling on love and compassion so that they might spontaneously arise in your daily practice.

Poems, Stanzas and Scriptural Passages

Below are inspirational verses from various traditions to help stimulate your own contemplation and journaling on love and compassion.

Christianity

Love is patient, love is kind;
It does not envy, it does not boast,
It is not proud, nor is it rude;
It is not self-seeking, nor easily angered,
It keeps no record of wrongs.
Love does not delight in evil,
But rejoices in the truth.
Love bears all things, believes all things,
Hopes all things, and endures all things.
Love never ends.
- St. Paul in his *First Letter to the Corinthians*

- - - - -

And God said to the soul:
I desired you before the world began.
I desire you now
As you desire me.
And where the desires of two come together
There love is perfected

HOW THE SOUL SPEAKS TO THE SOUL
Lord, you are my lover,
My longing,
My flowing stream,
My sun,
And I am your reflection.

HOW GOD ANSWERS THE SOUL
It is my nature that makes me love you often,

[iv] For additional information on this step, please refer to the book *InterSpiritual Meditation.* The following materials are provided to stimulate your journaling.

For I am love itself.
It is my longing that makes me love you intensely,
For I yearn to be loved from the heart.
It is my eternity that makes me love you long,
For I have no end.

- Mechthild of Madgeburg, from *Teachings of the Christian Mystics*, Edited byAndrew Harvey

Buddhism

May be a guide for those who journey on the road.
May I be a boat, a raft, a bridge
For those who wish to cross the water.

May I be an isle for those who yearn for land,
A lamp for those who long for light;
For all who need a resting place, a bed;
For those who need a servant, may I be their slave.

May I be the wishing jewel, the vase of wealth,
A word of power and the supreme healing,
May I be the tree of miracles,
For every being the abundant cow.

Thus, for everything that lives,
As far as are the limits of the sky,
May I be constantly their source of livelihood
Until they pass beyond all sorrow.

- *Way of the Bodhisattva, 3:18-20, 22*

Hinduism

Love is the firstborn,
Loftier than the Gods;
You, O Love, are the eldest of all,
Altogether mighty.
To you we pay homage!

Greater than the breadth
Of Earth and Heaven
Or of Waters and Fire,
You, O Love, are the eldest of all,
Altogether mighty.
To you we pay homage!

Greater than the quarters and directions,
The expanses and vistas of the sky,
You, O Love, are the eldest of all,
Altogether mighty.
To you we pay homage!

Greater than all things moving and inert,
Than the Ocean, O Passion,
You, O Love, are the eldest of all,
Altogether mighty.
To you we pay homage!

Beyond the reach of Wind or Fire,
The Sun or the Moon,
You, O Love, are the eldest of all,
Altogether mighty.
To you we pay homage!

In many a form of goodness, O Love,
You show your face.
Grant that these forms may penetrate
Within our hearts.
Send elsewhere all malice!
- *Atharva Veda IX: 2:19-21, 23-25*

Sufism

The sickness of love is not like any other;
Love is the astrolabe of God's mysteries.
Whether Love is from heaven or earth,
it points to God.
However I may try to explain it,
When faced with Love itself
I'm ashamed of my explanations.
Whatever the tongue can make clear,
Love's silence is better.

And though the pen wanted badly to write,
when it came to Love its nib split apart.
When it was the turn of the Intellect
To unfold the meaning of Love,
It stumbled like a donkey in the mud.
In the end only Love
Could explain itself
And what it is to be a lover.

Mathnawi, I, 110-111 of Jalaluddin Rumi,
translated by Camille and Kabir Helminski in *Rumi Daylight*

- - - - - -

My soul is a furnace
happy with the fire.
Love, too, is a furnace,
and ego its fuel.

Mathnawi, II, 1376-7, Quoted by Helminski in *Jewels of Rumi*

Judaism

You shall not take vengeance or bear a grudge against your kinsfolk.
Love your neighbor as yourself…
Leviticus 19:18, the "Great Commandment"

- - - - - -

The stranger who resides with you shall be to you as one of your citizens;
you shall love him as yourself, for you were strangers in the land of Egypt.
Leviticus 19:34

- - - - - -

That which is hateful to you, do not do to your fellow.
That is the whole Torah; the rest is the explanation; go and learn.
Talmud, Shabbat 31a, the "Great Principle"

Questions to Stimulate Contemplation and Journaling

The world's contemplative traditions often concur about the types of mental attributes and methods to be cultivated for generating compassion. Below, I have listed some of these along with questions to stimulate your journaling and contemplative regarding each. These attributes and methods include sympathy and empathy, equalizing self and others, realizing the interdependence between person happiness and the happiness of others, the natural law of reciprocity, the universal pervasiveness of love and compassion.

Your journal writings will help love and compassion to emerge even when we don't feel that way. They will help provide a focus for love and compassion for Step Four of InterSpiritual Meditation. First, you might begin by exploring answers to these questions.

What is your definition for love and compassion?

Do these arise solely from inside your self or are they a universal quality that you tap into?

Describe how love and compassion arise in you: Are they dependent on a desirable object or person. Or do they arise when you see someone who is suffering, in danger or deprived of their basic human rights?

Is your love and compassion conditional, or does it arise naturally and spontaneously without conditions?

How is your own health and happiness connected with the love and compassion others have for you?

How is the well-being and happiness of others intertwined with your own?

Do you gain greater happiness when you selfishly get what you want or when you help another person get what he or she needs?

Sympathy and Empathy

Are you able to sympathize with the suffering of others by relating it to your own experience?

Are you able to empathize heart to heart with others with a spontaneous wish to help relieve their suffering and bring them happiness?

Exchange and Equalize Self and Others

When you lack spontaneous compassion for a difficult person, have you tried changing places with them?

When you see the world through the eyes of another, are you better able to see the causes of their suffering and feel love and compassion toward them?

Are you able to objectively look at your own suffering and feel the same sympathy, empathy, love and compassion that you would feel for another person who is suffering?

What does it feel like when you put yourself in another's shoes to feel their suffering, to realize why they might be suffering, and why they might be acting negatively towards you?

What does it feel like when you "trade places" with others who are suffering and see the world through their eyes?

How are you able to see yourself in others and others in you? What changes to you observe in yourself when you see that we all share the challenges inherent in the human condition?

When you do have empathy, how are your negative feelings affected toward those you have aversion towards? Does this empathy motivate you to find ways to alleviate the causes of their internal pain or negative behavior?

How does this empathy help you to practice the Golden Rule, "Do unto others as you would have them do unto you?"

Interdependence and Universal Reciprocity

How do you perceive the causal and interdependent nature of things?

How do you understand the interdependence between personal happiness and the happiness of others?

How does interdependence entail reciprocity, whereby all things are serving the needs of others?

What is your way of describing the natural state of universal reciprocity?

How do you describe the inter-permeability between living beings?

What words might you use to describe or express the possible interrelationship between universal reciprocity and universal love and compassion?

Universal Essence

How is it possible that love and compassion could be essential qualities of the universe?

How would you relate love and compassion with your sense of God, ground of being or higher power.

Your Contemplative Practice

Please remember that the purpose of the above quotes and questions is to stimulate your writing in your journals. In your writing, please explore your own deepest personal insights as well as your beliefs that have been molded by your tradition, teachers, mentors or role models. You might also do additional research on the internet, in books and conversations with other teachers and students. Then, reflecting on your writings, create a brief summary that will serve as the contemplative focus for this step.

As you begin this step, say to yourself with conviction: "May I be Loving and Compassionate." This will serve not only a prayer, but also your self-directed challenge to actualize the qualities of love and compassion twenty-four hours a day, seven days a week for the rest of your life, indeed, your eternal existence. With this determination, engage in meditation to become loving and compassionate and to eliminate the negative states of mind that prevent you from actualizing these. In your contemplation, bring to mind the summary of your journal writings and vow to actualize these in your life. Here, in answer to our prayer, we open ourselves to the transformative power and support of the vast and untapped potential of consciousness, and our greatest potential.

STEP FIVE

MINDFULNESS

"MAY I BECOME MINDFUL THROUGH MY BREATHING"

Wherever I shine the lamplight of Divine breath,
there the difficulties of a whole world are resolve
The darkness which the earthly sun did not remove,
becomes through My breath a bright morning.

- Mathnawi I, 1941-2 of Jalaluddin Rumi,
translated by Camille and Kabir Helminski

STEP 5: MINDFULNESS –
"May I Become Mindful Through My Breathing"[v]

In many spiritual traditions, subtle breath is equated with spirit and the vital source of life. There are many types of meditations on breathing and these can be used for healing, stress reduction, physical strength, tranquility, equanimity, one-pointed concentration, transcendent states of consciousness, unity with the divine and for emptying the obstacles to wisdom, compassion and freedom. Breath meditations are often a prelude to deep states of meditative absorption and realization.

Breathing connects us to the interdependent reciprocal nature of all existence. For example, we breathe in the oxygen produced by plants and we exhale the carbon dioxide that plants need to survive. The microscopic living cells that compose our body are nourished by the oxygen we breathe in. The health of these cells is tantamount to the health of our body. In this way, breathing connects our inner and outer worlds.

The mental skill called "mindfulness" is often associated with Buddhism, but it also can be found either implicit or explicit in many other contemplative traditions. The term can include various attributes including the attention, recollection, concentration and observation, each of which carry slightly different connotations. The following quotes and questions are meant to stimulate your contemplation on these attributes of mindfulness and to help you create a focus on breath and breathing in a way that has personal meaning and benefit.

Poems, Stanzas and Scriptural Passages

Below are inspirational verses from various traditions to help stimulate your own contemplation and journaling for Step Five.

Buddhism

A *bhikkhu* having gone to the forest,
To the foot of a tree, or a solitary place,
Sits down cross-legged, the body erect,
And directs the mind to the object of mindfulness;
Then, with mindfulness, breathes in and breathes out:
Inhaling a long breath — "I inhale a long breath,"
Exhaling a long breath — "I exhale a long breath,"
Inhaling a short breath — "I inhale a short breath,"
Exhaling a short breath — "I exhale a short breath";
"Aware of this whole body of breath, I breathe in,"
"Aware of this whole body of breath, I breathe out,"
"Calming the process of breathing, I breathe in,"
"Calming the process of breathing, I breathe out,"
Thus does the *bhikkhu* train awareness.
- *Mahasatipatanasutta*

---

[v] For additional information on this step, please refer to the book *InterSpiritual Meditation*. The following materials are provided to stimulate your journaling.

Islam

Wherever I shine the lamplight of Divine breath,
there the difficulties of a whole world are resolve
The darkness which the earthly sun did not remove,
becomes through My breath a bright morning.

- *Mathnawi* I, 1941-2 of Jalaluddin Rumi
translated by Camille and Kabir Helminski in *Rumi Daylight*

Hinduism

Praise to your coming and your going,
Breath,
Praise to your rising and your settling,
Breath!

Praise to you, Breath of Life,
For both breathing in and out!
For turning to this side and to that,
Praise to all of you, everywhere!

Breath of Life, grant your blessed form
To us that we may live!
Give us your healing power!

The Breath of Life cares for all beings
Like a parent their child;
Master of all life, breathing or not.

We breathe in, we breathe out,
Even within the womb.
Quickened and enlivened by you,
And you bring us to birth!

Breath of Life, please do not forsake me.
You are, indeed, everything that I am.
As the embryo of all potential,
I bind myself to you that I may live!
- *Atharva Veda* XI, 4:1-10, 14, 26

Christianity

Truly, truly, I say unto you,
Except a person be born
Of water and of the spirit-breath,
They cannot enter into the kingdom of God.
- John 3:5

Judaism

The heavens are shaped by Yah's Word,
Yah's breath gives life to all its being.
- Psalms 33:6

- - - -

The Sovereign Lord says to these bones:
I will make breath enter you,
And you will come to life.
- Ezekiel 37:5

- - - -

And *Y-H-V-H*, God, formed the human, of the dust from the soil,
he blew into his nostrils the breath of life and
the human became a human being.
- Genesis 2:7

Taoism

Empty yourself of everything.
Let the mind become still.
The ten thousand things rise and fall
While the Self watches their return.
They grow and flourish
And then return to the source.
Returning to the source is stillness,
Which is the way of nature.
- Lao Tzu, *Tao Te Ching, 16*

Questions to Stimulate Contemplation and Journaling

The teachings of the world's contemplative traditions often concur regarding the seminal importance of breath and breathing. Below, I have listed six of the mental attributes to be cultivated around the practice of breathing and focus on breath. These include body position, attention, concentrated focus, patience, perseverance, inner observation or vigilance and recollection.

The questions relating to each of these six mental attributes are meant to help you cultivate mindfulness through breathing. Please journal your thoughts and insights as a foundation for your own meditation.

Body Position

Contemplation and meditation can take place in a variety of body positions including sitting cross-legged on a cushion, sitting on a chair, walking, running, swimming, bicycling or laying down.

Why is the right body position important for meditation?

What is the position (or positions) that helps you to stay alert, focused and yet relaxed?

Why is this position better than the others?

Attention

Full attention to the object or purpose of meditation is important in many traditions and types of meditation.

Generally, do you find it challenging to focus your attention on one thing or task?

Is it easier for you to focus your attention on breath, a syllable, an image, a prayer, a physical movement, and sacred symbol or perhaps a universal truth?

What resistance or challenges do you experience when you try to focus your attention?

What are the sacred and secular benefits of cultivating focused attention?

Are you willing to devote the your time and effort to cultivating attention?

How often are you willing to work at developing the attribute of focused attention?

Concentrated Focus on Breath and Breathing

Concentration on breath and breathing is of seminal importance in many types of meditation as well as spiritual practice.

What does breath mean to you? Is it simply the air that you breathe in and out? Does breath have a sacred significance?

In relation to your personal spiritual or scientific orientation, how do understand breath beyond its simple physical necessity for daily life?

What types of physical and mental feelings or sensations emerge for you when you focus on your breathing?

What are the beneficial effects of focused breathing on your mind and body?

How does focus on breathing in and out help you to become calm and present in the moment?

How does focus on breath help you to deepen and expand your life experience both in meditation, in relationships, in work and in sports, etc?

Patience

In mindfulness practice, patience does not refer to forbearance towards other people but to the inner workings of our own mind. If we try too hard with the unrealistic expectation of quick results, the benefits of meditation will elude us. Without patience, meditation itself can be a stressful activity.

How do you define the meaning of patience?

Do you find yourself becoming impatient when it is hard to focus on your breathing?

Do you become impatient when the tranquility of meditation eludes you?

What is the effect of impatience in your meditation?

What method do you use in your meditation to cultivate patience?

How would you describe the result of approaching meditation with patience rather than worrying that you won't immediately gain the results you expect?

Inner Observation or Vigilance

Non-judgmental observation and vigilance of the internal mental and physical feelings, perceptions, sensations, emotions, memories and desires is the ally of focused concentration. Without inner vigilance, our minds will wander aimlessly and our physical sensations will distract us. Distractions will prevent us from achieving calm meditational focus.

Why should you cultivate the capacity to observe the inner workings of your mind and body?

What are the benefits of inner observation and vigilance?

Are you committed to developing the capacity for inner observation and vigilance?

How do you understand the capacity of your mind for the parallel processing of thoughts, emotions, memory and possibly even projections, along with simultaneous observation of these mental events?

What is your experience in your attempts to cultivate inner observation and vigilance?

Describe the quality of your observation and vigilance, your ability to notice the emergence of mental events, and your ability to return to the object of meditation?

Recollection

Mental and physical distractions often impede our continued focus on the object or purpose of meditation. Therefore, in order to refocus our minds after inevitable distractions, we cultivate our capacity to recollect, remember and return to the object or purpose of our meditation.

What is the value in being able to recollect or remember the object of meditation?

How would you describe your internal experience when you try to remember the object of meditation, for example, your breath, a syllable, a prayer or an image?

How is your recollection impeded by the incessant arising of thoughts, emotions, sensations and memories?

How can the cultivation of all these attributes of mindfulness improve your meditation?

How does mindful breathing help you to achieve mental calm and focus in daily life?

Your Meditative Practice

Please remember that the purpose of the above quotes and questions is to stimulate your writing in your journals. In your writing, please explore your own deepest personal insights as well as your beliefs that have been molded by your tradition, teachers, mentors or role models. You might also do additional research on the internet, in books and through conversations with other teachers and students. Then, reflecting on your writings, create a brief summary that will be your contemplative focus for this step.

What type of breathing practice will you develop? How will you cultivate the attributes listed above?

As you begin this step, say to yourself with conviction: "May I be Mindful through my Breathing." This will serve not only as a prayer, but also your self-directed challenge to actualize mindfulness whether awake or sleeping. With this determination, engage in meditation to become mindful and to eliminate the negative states of mind that prevent you from actualizing the attributes of mindfulness.

In your contemplation, bring to mind the summary of your journal writings and vow to actualize these in your life. Here, in answer to our prayer, we open ourselves to the transformative power and support of the vast and untapped potential of consciousness and our greatest potential.

STEP SIX

MEDITATION

"MAY I BECOME WISE THROUGH MY MEDITATION"

Before heaven and earth
There was something nebulous
silent isolated
unchanging and alone
eternal
the Mother of All Things
I do not know its name
I call it Tao.

- Tao Te Ching

STEP 6: MEDITATION

"May I Become Wise Through My Meditation"[vi]

By way of review and context, please recall that each of the first four steps in this seven step process are contemplative. That is, they require deep and calm conceptual consideration regarding our motivation, transformation, gratitude and compassionate intention. However, Step Five is called "meditative" because it entails and non-conceptual focus on our breath along with the capacity to observe distractions, returning to the meditative object, at this point our breath, and sustain our tranquil concentration. It is called "meditative" because there is no conceptualization taking place. Each of these steps gradually help to prepare our minds for Step Six.

In many traditions, the primary purpose of meditation is to cultivate non-conceptual wisdom. It is often regarded as a direct insight into the truth of existence and/or a state of unity with God or a sacred state of being. Wisdom cultivated through meditation is the foundation for personal liberation as well as wise, loving and compassionate service in the world. Although each spiritual tradition may have its own name for the ultimate reality, its own specified goals, nevertheless there are similarities in the meditative processes leading to that goal. Because InterSpiritual Meditation is non-sectarian and inclusive, it does not specify a metaphysical goal. Rather it provides a universal process to help each person develop and actualize their own spiritual goal or purpose. In so doing, we celebrate the diversity of the profound contemplative states of consciousness found throughout the world.

The following poems, stanzas and scriptural passages are provided to help you journal the purpose and focus of your meditation. Your meditation might be a continuation of mindful breathing in Step Five, or it might come from a single tradition or from a variety of traditions you have previously studied and have experience practicing. This is your opportunity to articulate, summarize and practice the meditation of your choosing. If you have collected inspirational writings from other sources, please add these to you journal.

Poems, Stanzas and Scriptural Passages

Below are inspirational verses from various traditions to help stimulate your own contemplation and journaling for this, Step Six.

Christianity

If you want to pray,
Enter your inner room,
Close the door,
And pray to your Father in secret,
And your Father who sees in secret
Will reward you.
- Mathew 6:6[vii]

[vi] For additional information on this step, please refer to the book *InterSpiritual Meditation*. The following materials are provided to stimulate your journaling.

[vii] This is the scriptural source for Centering Prayer, or Contemplative Prayer, as taught by Father Thomas Keating.

For He can well be loved, but he cannot be thought. By love he can be grasped and held, but by thought, neither grasped nor held. And therefore, though it may be good at times to think specifically of the kindness and excellence of God, and though this may be a light and a part of contemplation, all the same, in the work of contemplation itself, it must be cast down and covered with a cloud of forgetting. And you must step above it stoutly but deftly, with a devout and delightful stirring of love, and struggle to pierce that darkness above you; and beat on that thick cloud of unknowing with a sharp dart of longing love, and do not give up, whatever happens.

- The Cloud of Unknowing, author unknown

- - - - - -

Let nothing disturb you;
Let nothing make you afraid;
All things pass;
But God is unchanging'
Patience
is enough for everything.
You who have God
lack nothing.
God alone is sufficient.
- Teresa of Avila

- - - - - -

Ah blessed absence of God,
How lovingly I am bound to you!
You strengthen my will in its pain
And make dear to me
The long hard wait in my poor body.
The nearer I come to you,
The more wonderfully and abundantly
God comes upon me.
In pride, alas, I can easily lose you,
But in the depths of pure humility, O Lord,
I cannot fall away from you.
For the deeper I fall, the sweeter you taste.

- Mechthild of Magdeburg, Translated by Oliver Davies

Buddhism

Just as a bird with undeveloped
Wings cannot fly in the sky,
Those without the power of higher perception
Cannot work for the good of living beings.
The merit gained in a single day
By one who possess higher perception
Cannot be gained even in a hundred lifetimes

By one without such higher perception.
Those who want swiftly to complete
The collections for full enlightenment
Will accomplish higher perception
Through effort, not through laziness.

Without the attainment of calm abiding,
Higher perception will not occur.
Therefore make a repeated effort
To accomplish calm abiding.

When the practitioner has gained calm abiding,
Higher perception will also be gained,
But without practice of the perfection of wisdom,
The obstructions will not come to an end.
(Atisha , Lamp for the Path to Enlightenment)

Hinduism

"One who meditates
On contemplation as Brahman,
Their freedom will extend to
The limits of the realm of contemplation ..."
"But, sir, is there anything greater than contemplation?"
"Yes, there is something greater than contemplation."
"Then please, sir, tell me about it!"

"Wisdom, verily, is greater than contemplation.
For by wisdom one knows heaven and earth.
Air and atmosphere, water and fire,
Gods, human beings, and animals, grass and trees,
Right and wrong, true and false, pleasant and unpleasant,
Food and drink, this world and the other . . .
All these are known by wisdom.
Meditate on wisdom.

"One who meditates on wisdom as Brahman,
Attains the worlds of wisdom and of knowledge.
Their freedom will extend to the limits of the realm of wisdom,
One who meditates on wisdom as Brahman."
- *Chandogya Upanishad* VII, 6:1-7:2

Sufism

Listen, O drop, give yourself up without regret,
        and in exchange gain the Ocean.
Listen, O drop, bestow upon yourself this honor,
        and in the arms of the Sea be secure.
Who indeed should be so fortunate?
        An Ocean wooing a drop!

In God's name, in God's name, sell and buy at once!
Give a drop, and take this Sea full of pearls.

- Mathnawi, IV, 2619-2622, translated by Camille and Kabir Helminski, Jewels of Remembrance

- - - - - -

Let your heart be in such a state that the existence or non-existence of anything is the same—that is, let there be no dichotomy of positive and negative. Then sit alone in a quiet place, free of any task or preoccupation, be it the reciting of the Qur'an, thinking about its meaning, concern over the dictates of religion, or what you have read in books—let nothing besides God enter the mind. Once you are seated in this manner, start to pronounce with your tongue, "Allah, Allah" keeping your thought on it.

Practice this continuously and without interruption; you will reach a point when the motion of the tongue will cease, and it will appear as if the word just flows from it spontaneously. You go on in this way until every trace of the tongue movement disappears while the heart registers the thought or the idea of the word.

As you continue with this invocation, there will come a time when the word will leave the heart completely. Only the palpable essence or reality of the name will remain, binding itself ineluctably to the heart.

Up to this point everything will have been dependent on your own conscious will; the divine bliss and enlightenment that may follow have nothing to do with your conscious will or choice. What you have done so far is to open the window, as it were. You have laid yourself exposed to what God may breathe upon you, as He has done upon his prophets and saints.

If you follow what is said above, you can be sure that the light of Truth will dawn upon your heart. At first intermittently, like flashes of lightning, it will come and go. Sometimes when it comes back it may stay longer than other times. Sometimes it may stay only briefly.

- Al-Ghazali, Quoted by Kabir Helminski in *Meditations for InterSpiritual Wisdom*

- - - - - -

What does it mean to learn the knowledge of God's Unity?
To consume yourself in the presence of the One.
If you wish to shine like day,
burn up the night of self-existence.
Dissolve in the Being who is everything.
You grabbed hold of "I" and "we,"
and this dualism is your ruin.

- *Mathnawi* I, 3009-12 of Jalaluddin Rumi,
translated by Camille and Kabir Helminski in *Rumi Daylight*

Taoism

Before heaven and earth
There was something nebulous
silent isolated
unchanging and alone
eternal
the Mother of All Things
I do not know its name
I call it Tao.
- *Tao Te Ching*

Secular

Those who dwell among the beauties and mysteries of the earth are never alone
or weary of life…Those who contemplate the beauty of the earth find reserves of
strength that will endure as long as life lasts.
- Rachel Carson, *The Sense of Wonder*

Questions to Stimulate Your Contemplation and Journaling on Meditation

Mature meditators often report that it has taken them may years before they regularly experience the
fruits of their practice. The process of meditation, they say, is not always like a "spiritual jacuzzi." Not
only do we need to know the techniques and formulas for our chosen meditation, but we need strong
and abiding rationale, faith, perseverance and devotion for sustaining our practice.

Whether our meditation is proscribed by a teacher, a tradition or of your own design, it is important for
you to own it, so to speak, and take personal responsibility for it. It is unrealistic to expect that the
meditation will be done to you, for you and that sublime experiences will happen automatically without
your full commitment and engagement. Meditation is an inner career that to accompany us throughout
out lives. Our mind is like a garden and meditation is the process we use to tend, nurture and make it
healthy.

The world's contemplative traditions often concur about the general processes of meditation and the
mental attributes to be cultivated in order to develop a mature practice. The following questions are
posed to stimulate your contemplative journaling. Your journal writings will help you formulate your
own personal focus for this step. In developing or refining your meditation, these questions might help
you gain clarity, confidence and consistency.

Refining Your Expectations for Meditation

How would you describe the purpose of your meditation? For example do you meditate to actualize
your own innate potential and/or to acquire the attributes of a higher power?

What are the fundamental beliefs you bring into this meditation regarding, for example, the nature
of your being, a higher power and the existence of God, or even the nature of the universe?

How do you define or describe your sense of the absolute truth, for example, God, Allah, Brahman,
the Tao, Universal Consciousness and Primordial Energy?

How do you define or describe the nature of your essential being: self, soul or spirit, mind, or perhaps something different?

What spiritual benefits do you hope for from meditation?

What is the state-of-being you hope will arise from meditation?

What psychological, emotional or physical benefits do you hope will come from meditation?

What changes in your relationships and career do you hope will come from meditating?

Do you have full confidence that your meditation can help achieve the results you hope for?

Do you have full confidence in the teacher or tradition that is the source of your meditation?

How would you describe your own personal responsibility in the development and practice of your meditation?

Choosing the Right Meditation for You

As you attempt to refine your present meditation or find a meditation that is best for you, the following types of meditation might help you gain clarity. These questions are not meant to lead you to any general or particular answer, nor to imply that there is a right answer for all people, but to aid you in uncovering the answer most appropriate and relevant for you at this time.

Tranquil Focus

Tranquil focus is a necessary condition for meditation.

What type of meditation will help you gain tranquil focus? Will it involve movement (like Yoga, Tai Chi, Chi Gong, walking, dancing or running? Will it require silence? Will it be better with a group or alone?

What is the best point of focus of your meditation? For example, is it your breath, unity, inter-being-ness, emptiness, God, Allah, Brahman, the Tao, nature, love, remembrance, prayer?

Insight

Non-conceptual direct insight and sense of unity is the hallmark of many meditations.

How would you describe the sacred truth or divine state of being that you meditation will help you to realize directly?

Via Positiva and *Via Negativa*

Meditative traditions are often categorized as being either *via positiva* (cataphatic)and *via negativa* (apophatic). The first type, *via positiva*, connotes the accumulation of qualities the intended goal. The second, *via negativa*, implies eliminating the inner obstacles that prevent us from actualizing the goal, for example, by emptying ourselves of a false or limited sense of self. Some traditions emphasize one over another while some combine both.

When you meditate, how would you describe your inner methodology? For example, is your goal to empty out the negative contents of your consciousness so that it can be filled up by the divine or sacred?

Bliss

Are you hoping that your meditation will yield a feeling of bliss?

Would the feeling of bliss make you feel that you are getting somewhere in you meditation?

Is it possible that bliss is just a physical endorphin-like sensation that occurs when the mind is focused? Or might there be a kind of bliss consciousness that is not connected to a physical cause?

Is it possible that bliss might be a distraction from a more profound purpose? If so, what is the antidote to this type of distraction?

Equanimity

Are you hoping for a state of deep calm and equanimity from your meditation?

How do you relate the terms happiness, equanimity, and calm? Are they interchangeable, mutually inclusive, or independent of each other?

Do you fear equanimity because it might extinguish the vibrant highs and lows of life?

Unity or Oneness

What do the terms "unity" and "oneness" mean to you?

How do you relate to the terms unity and oneness? Are they states of mind or being that you would like to experience or achieve in meditation?

Your Contemplative Practice

Please remember that the purpose of the above quotes and questions is to stimulate your writing in your journals. In your writing, please explore your own deepest personal insights as well as your beliefs that have been molded by your tradition, teachers, mentors, or role models. You might also do additional research on the internet, in books and conversations with other teachers and students. Then, reflecting on your writings, create a brief summary that will be the contemplative focus for this step.

As you begin this step, say to yourself with conviction: "May I become Wise Through My Meditation." This will serve not only as a prayer, but also your self-directed challenge to enter into meditation in order to gain the insight and wisdom to serve the highest purposes of all beings. With this determination, we engage in our meditation to realize its highest benefits. Before entering into your meditation bring to mind the summary of your journal writings and vow to actualize them.

Here, in answer to our prayer, we open ourselves to the transformative power and support of the vast and untapped potential of consciousness and your personal sense of the divine of higher power.

Step Seven

Dedication

"MAY I SERVE ALL BEINGS"

And now as long as space endures,

As long as there are beings to be found,

May I continue likewise to remain

To drive away the sorrows of the world.

—Bodhicharyavatara 10:5526

76

STEP 7: DEDICATION

"May I be in Service to All Beings"[viii]

As we gradually begin to emerge from our meditation we rededicate ourselves to wise, loving and compassionate service to others. We do this with the implicit understanding that our own wellbeing is inextricably intertwined with our vow to help others. We visualize the coming days and the inevitable challenges we have with certain situations and people. Visualizing these, we preload, so to speak, the compassionate wisdom of our meditation into those future moments so we are prepared to meet them with the grace of our inner purpose. By doing this, we transform our approach to the everyday stresses of life. In order for our meditation to stay with us and be of lasting benefit, it is very important that we end our session with our commitment to infuse each moment of the coming days with gratitude, compassion, mindful breathing and wisdom gained through meditation.

Poems, Stanzas and Scriptural Passages

Below are inspirational verses from various traditions to help stimulate your own contemplation and journaling for Step Seven.

Christianity

Lord, make me an instrument of your peace,
Where there is hatred, let me sow love;
where there is injury, pardon;
where there is doubt, faith;
where there is despair, hope;
where there is darkness, light;
where there is sadness, joy;

Divine Master, grant that I
may not so much seek to be consoled as to console;
to be understood as to understand;
to be loved as to love.

For it is in giving that we receive;
it is in pardoning that we are pardoned;
and it is in dying that we are born to eternal life.
- St. Francis of Assisi

Buddhism

And now as long as space endures,
As long as there are beings to be found,
May I continue likewise to remain
To drive away the sorrows of the world.
- Shantideva, *Way of the Bodhisattva, 10:55*

[viii] For additional information on this step, please refer to the book *InterSpiritual Meditation.* The following materials are provided to stimulate your journaling.

Native American

We have come on a good road
Of loving one another
And sticking by one another.
At this time we will disperse,
So keep the good work
And love one another.
That is the road that we came from,
The road of life,
Nothing but good,
And have strong will power
To do all this.
And all this, it will be so.
Slow Buffalo, Lakota Chief

O Great Spirit, whose voice I hear in the wind and whose breath gives life to all the world, hear me. I come before you, one of your many children. I am weak and small. I need your strength and wisdom. Let me walk in beauty and make my eyes ever behold the red and purple sunset; my ears sharp so I may hear your voice. Make me wise, so I may learn the things you have taught my people; the lessons you have hidden under every rock and leaf. I seek strength not to be superior to others, but to come to you with clean hands and straight eyes, so whenever life fades, like the fading sunset, my spirit will come to you without shame.
- *Chief Yellow Lark Blackfoot*

Judaism

There is holiness when we strive to be true to the best we know.
There is holiness when we are kind to someone who cannot
possibly be of service to us.
There is holiness when we promote family harmony.
There is holiness when we forget what divides us and remember
what unites us.
There is holiness when we love truly and honestly and unselfishly.
There is holiness when we remember the lonely and bring cheer
into a dark corner.

- Kedushah prayer

Sufism

Abandon this sly plotting for a while:
live free a few moments before you die.

- Mathnawi, VI, 4444 of Jalaluddin Rumi,
translated by Camille and Kabir Helminski in Jewels of Remembrance

The Messenger of good tidings said, speaking symbolically,
"Die before you die, generous ones,
even as I have died before death
and brought this reminder from Beyond."
Become the resurrection of the spirit,
so you may experience the resurrection:
this becoming is necessary for seeing and knowing
the real nature of anything.
Until you become it, you will not know it completely,
whether it be light or darkness.
If you become Reason, you will know Reason perfectly;
if you become Love, you will know Love's flaming wick.

- Mathnawi, VI, 754-758 of Jalaluddin Rumi,

translated by Camille and Kabir Helminski in Jewels of Remembrance

Questions to Stimulate Contemplation and Journaling on Your Dedication

The world's contemplative traditions concur on the importance of dedication. Here are a series of questions to stimulate your journaling on your personal dedication.

What qualities and attributes of this entire meditation will you bring into the coming days? How will you carry these forward with you in each moment?

What are the relationships and who are the people in your life with whom your experience stress, unhappiness, unease and even anger? How will you bring the qualities and attributes of this meditation into your relationship with them?

What are the situations in which you become stressed, impatient, unhappy and angry? How will you bring the attributes of this meditation into those situations?

What are the reoccurring worries in your life, whether they are people, finances, job, relationships or uncertainty over the future? How will you apply this meditation as an antidote to these?

How will you be mindful of, and monitor your own negative inner states mind that arise in these circumstances?

Your Contemplative Practice

Please remember that the purpose of the above quotes and questions is to stimulate your writing in your journals. In your writing, please explore your own deepest personal conclusions as well as your beliefs that have been molded by your tradition, teachers, mentors, or role models. You might also do additional research on the internet, in books and conversations with other teachers and students. Then, reflecting on your writings, create a brief summary that will be the contemplative focus for this step.

As you begin this step, say to yourself with conviction: "May I be in Service to All Beings." This will serve not only as a prayer, but also your commitment to apply the personal benefits of meditation to the sustainable happiness of all beings, and to utilize the wisdom gained in meditation to alleviate their suffering. As you enter into this final step in our meditation, bring to mind the summary of your journal writings and vow to actualize them.

YOUR INTERSPIRITUAL MEDITATION SESSION

Beginning Your
InterSpiritual Meditation Practice[ix]

InterSpiritual Consciousness

The experience at the Snowmass Conference was truly critical for me. It showed me a possibility I had never considered before—that people of different faiths could come together to share an experience of profound spiritual depth. During that silent meditation, which included a Hindu swami of the Vedanta tradition, an Eastern Orthodox Christian priest, a Hasidic Jew, and a Muslim Sufi, it was clear to me that a group consciousness was being created by us, even in the silence. It is this consciousness that I now tend to think of as an InterSpiritual Consciousness. Let me give you an example that may hit a little closer to home:

Imagine you are in a room with a group of angry people, perhaps a tension filled boardroom, or in an airport terminal when your flight has just been cancelled. Is it really necessary to say anything for the anger and frustration to be communicated? We have all been in these situations, and we all know that the group-feeling is communicated, even without words. This is why we say things like, 'You could cut the tension with a knife,' because the feeling is almost tangible.

Likewise, there are shared environments of excitement, as at sporting events and concerts, joy and love in gatherings of friends and family, inexplicable empathy between strangers in times of danger; but we don't generally consider the implications of this sharing. We take it for granted, which is to say that we participate in these 'sharings' unconsciously. But what if we didn't? What if we gathered together with the conscious intention of cultivating love and harmony through a shared experience of group meditation? What if people of different faiths could join together in an all-inclusive meditation process? Is it possible that something might be shared between them, a new and deeper intimacy created? I believe this is precisely what can result.

If the sensitivity of our individual consciousness is not confined to particular parts of our bodies, if it extends in some way beyond our bodies, and further, if in meditation we all simultaneously give rise to a shared intention, isn't it possible then that individual consciousness may fuse with the consciousness of other individuals to form a larger group consciousness? As I said before, this idea was a "breakthrough" for me, but not because I hadn't already experienced this in meditation and practice with other Buddhists, but because I had never considered it possible with people of different faiths! The truth is, many spiritual traditions have long been aware of and have even cultivated group consciousness, but not many have extended it to the sharing of intentions *InterSpiritually,* that is to say, with persons of other faiths, as we are beginning to do today.

Nor was this a breakthrough for me alone, or else I might be suspected of fooling myself. But some of my other colleagues at the Snowmass Conference had experienced the same phenomenon. It was something that happened in the silence of shared periods of meditation and subsequent dialogues, something pointed out by Father Keating and repeated by Swami Atmarupananda in the book *The Common Heart:*

[ix] Originally appearing in Bastian, Edward W. *InterSpiritual Meditation: A Seven-Step Process from the World's Spiritual Traditions.* Santa Barbara, CA: Spiritual Paths Publishing, 2010.

[W]hen the dialogue [following our meditation] is good, we share an experience of flowing with a higher intelligence; our individual understanding seems uplifted into a collective sharing with something higher. That is how Father Tom [Keating] expressed it in our last meeting. In a sense, this is the most important aspect of dialogue. It doesn't always happen, but when it does, there is nothing like it. When we are immersed in the wisdom of the collective sharing, a higher understanding descends on all of the individuals.

The "dialogue" Father Keating and Swami Atmarupananda are talking about is not merely the verbal dialogue of our group discussion sessions, but also that of our silent meditations together. This is what we called, "the silent dialogue," which was every bit as enriching as the group discussions. Indeed, one participant, a Calvinist Christian minister, Rev. Don Postema, said of one of our silent meditation sessions:

There was truly a profound connection without words. And I remember that during one of those silent sessions in Cohasset [Massachusetts, where the seventh Snowmass Conference took place], I had a profound experience of the Presence of Jesus; my own experience of Christianity was strengthened through sharing meditation with folks of different spiritual traditions!

From this we can also see that even as we join together to create a group consciousness, individual experiences of profound depth are not hindered, and may even be enhanced. This is an important part of the InterSpiritual Meditation process, for even as we are sharing the process itself, and even as we may be creating a group consciousness, we are still using the language and basic practices of our own traditions. Thus, highly unique insights may occur and one may become more deeply grounded in one's own tradition.

Keep this in mind as you begin your practice of InterSpiritual Meditation. Though you may be starting your exploration of this process alone, or for your own personal development, look for opportunities to share it with others, especially those who may be pursuing different spiritual paths, or doing different meditation techniques. For the sharing of an InterSpiritual Consciousness is one of the the primary purposes of this process, and the means by which we may help to bring a little more peace to our fractured world.

Getting Started

So how does one begin a meditation practice? Obviously, we need to start small and begin at the beginning. After all, what mathematician ever started out with Calculus? First there was simple addition and subtraction, then division, then the multiplication tables. These are the foundations upon which the future mathematician builds their knowledge, gradually increasing their skill and competence in applying them year after year.

Of course, meditation does not require so much preliminary knowledge, but a mature meditation practice does take time to develop and has certain basic features that must be understood first. Like any other discipline, meditation takes dedication, time, patience, and work in order to bear fruit. Therefore, I want to discuss the context in which meditation is usually done, and some of the preliminaries to meditation practice.

Spiritual Traditions and Teachers

If you do not have a particular meditation practice, or do not belong to an established spiritual tradition, it might be helpful to explore the various meditation resources in this section of the book, "Meditations for InterSpiritual Practice." However, if you are actively looking for a path or a teacher, I would encourage you to use the utmost discretion and discernment in making this decision. Take your time and allow yourself to think it through thoroughly. As long as this isn't an avoidance tactic (or a habitual fear of commitment), diligence and perspicacity are advisable. Your spiritual future depends on making good and thoughtful decisions.

Once you have made an informed decision about your path, it is equally important to stay focused within a specific tradition until you have learned it well. Then you will be better prepared to explore the different aspects of meditation in other traditions. Although meditation practices across traditions share many basic features, there are also important nuances to their presentation and practice that can have a profound impact on the meditator. Keep this in mind as you explore the practices provided here.

Spiritual traditions are more than just their meditation practices; they are entire 'cultures' with unique rituals and customs, approaches and beliefs, and very particular paths to human transformation. So as you explore, try to do so as a traveler entering an indigenous village, treading carefully and with respect, approaching everything with 'beginner's mind.'

Why should you have a meditation teacher? Like many other life disciplines, it is helpful to refine our knowledge and practice by working with a good teacher within a well-established tradition. Meditation can be a long, slow process, and it is valuable to have someone with whom we can check our progress—and sometimes, our fantasies. Occasionally we cling to fantastic experiences that arise in our meditation and try to repeat these experiences again and again. While these experiences can be enthralling, they are often just distractions, the illusory projections of our own minds. It is also possible that you might have an experience that is unsettling and disorienting. A good teacher can let you know when you are on the right track, and help you to find balance and perspective again after potentially destabilizing experiences.

With regard to teachers, a great Hindu swami once said to me, "Because it is the disciple who must determine the 'guruness' of the guru, the disciple is actually the guru of the guru." My own teacher, Geshe Sopa, occasionally quoted the Buddha who said something along these lines: 'Don't put all your trust in the charisma of a teacher, but judge their living example. Still, don't have faith in this example alone, but pay attention to the wisdom of their words. Don't focus on the surface meaning of the words, but examine their deeper meaning. And don't stop your inquiry with the apparent or explicit meaning, but contemplate deeply the hidden or implicit meaning."

Geshe Sopa also quoted another saying of the Buddha as well: "Don't take my teachings on faith; rather, you should test the meanings like a goldsmith who assays the quality of the gold. You should rub it, cut it, burn it, and taste it." Faith based on a thorough discernment is more durable, and more sustainable. In the end, each of us must authenticate and actualize the teachings of any tradition through our own experience.

Postures and Environment

It is helpful to create an environment and maintain a body posture that is conducive for meditation. Before beginning the InterSpiritual Meditation process, you may want to light a candle or burn some incense to honor the beginning of the session. You should take a posture that is at once comfortable and stable; this might be cross-legged on a cushion on the floor, or on a chair with your back straight (not rigid) and your feet flat on the floor. Often, various meditative traditions have their own recommended postures; if you are not aware of them, these instructions will do fine for now. You might want to place your hands gently on your lap, or simply palms down on the tops of your thighs, roughly equidistant between your hip-joint and knees. You should feel relaxed within your body and fully present in this place.

At this point, you might adjust your gaze downward, gently closing your eyes until there is just a thin crack of light coming in. Begin inhaling and exhaling softly and evenly through your nose. Place the tip of your tongue on the roof of your mouth just behind your upper front teeth while your lips are kept gently together. Breathing easily, simply relax into the silence.

Lastly, you might want to place a small clock within site of your downward gaze so you can time your session. The seven parts of the InterSpiritual Meditation process outlined below have individual recommended time increments for a thirty-minute session of meditation.

Solo and Group Practice

The seven-part process of InterSpiritual Meditation provides a framework for individual and group practice. If you are using this process to guide an InterSpiritual group of meditators, I encourage you to begin the sessions together with a minimum of words. Let the shared silence be the connecting medium between you. Likewise, as you enter each individual step of the process, introduce that step with just a few words that indicate the purpose of the next few minutes, or with an experienced group who knows the process, you might simply use a small bell or gong to indicate the movement from one step to the next.

If you are doing this practice on your own, in the beginning it might be useful to follow the process in the order and time sequence in which it is presently arranged. Then, once you are familiar with each of the elements, you might customize it according to your own preferences. My goal is not to proscribe a rigid dogma, but to lay out the elements of a mature process for you to experience, experiment with, and integrate into your own personal practice.

Your personal journal is an important element in the creation of your seven-step meditation. It is important that you create a brief summary of your journal writings for each of the. Your writings can include the lessons from your teacher, a tradition you find helpful or a deep life experience. Your writings will also contain the perspectives you have learned by working through the lenses of your personal spiritual styles. These brief summaries will help provide content, focus and purpose for each step. Once you become accustomed to the process, the seven steps of InterSpiritual meditation will begin to flow easily on their own.

The InterSpiritual Meditation Process

The following is an outline of the seven steps and suggested times for each step. The words below can help you provide verbal guidance to yourself and others you might be leading. While the attributes for each step are listed below, they needn't all be stated as the focus for each step. They are just reminders of the contemplative content you will have written about in your personal journal. As you begin each step, you can choose the attributes that are most pertinent at this moment in the development of your practice.

1. Step One – Motivation (3 Minutes)

"May I Be Healthy and Happy"

In order to achieve anything significant in our lives—whether in our careers, sports, or relationships—we must have the proper motivation. Likewise, a lifelong spiritual practice also requires strong and unwavering motivation. In this first step, we establish our motivation and prayers for physical, emotional, mental, and spiritual healing, leading to sustainable happiness. To help us persevere, we begin each session by contemplating our own personal reasons and experiences that have brought us here.

> *a. Mind*
> *b. Body*
> *c. Spirit*

2. Step Two – Gratitude (3 Minutes)

"May I Be Grateful for Life's Many Gifts"

There is so much for which we can be grateful: our environment that gives us life and sustains us, life's challenges that enable us to grow, to become compassionate and wise, our ancestors and loved ones, our teachers and mentors. Whenever we learn to perform a new task, we depend on the example of others to guide us. This is especially true in spiritual practice when we invoke, remember, and honor the presence of our teachers, mentors, the saints, prophets, and founders of our respective traditions, and not least, God or the sacred dimension. We visualize and invite them to join us; we pray for their help that we might help others; and we thank them for all they have done for us. We also look gratefully on the difficulties and challenges of our lives for these help us to grow in wisdom and empathy for ourselves and others. In this step, we can also invoke the infinite potential that lies within our own consciousness, a potential for wisdom, compassion, and health. We invoke all these with deep gratitude.

> *a. Remembrance*
> *b. Thankfulness*
> *c. Trust and Faith*
> *d. Devotion*
> *e. Prayer*
> *f. Offering*
> *g. Sacrifice*

3. Step Three – Transformation (3 Minutes)

"May I Be Transformed Into My Highest Ideal"

In order to improve ourselves—whether professionally, in academics, athletics, ethics, in relationships, or spiritually—we must develop a clear image of that which we would like to become. Then we must be honest about our present condition, giving ourselves a personal 'reality check' with regard to our present inadequacies and the ways in which we would like to improve. We must admit that there is something wrong, something unsatisfactory in our lives, areas that we would like to improve, and make a promise to ourselves that we will strive to transform ourselves into the beings we most sincerely want to become. Without investing in debilitating guilt, we forgive ourselves (and others) for any part we (or they) might have played in our present situation. We renounce our attachment to the habits, desires, and behaviors that do not serve our highest ideals. Finally, we open ourselves to love, the universal healing and transformative agent for all beings everywhere. We are now ready to embark on the meditative practices required to acquire the qualities we desire and to eliminate the obstacles in our path.

> a. *Visualizing the Ideal*
> b. *Honest Self-Assessment*
> c. *Confession*
> d. *Remorse*
> e. *Forgiveness*
> f. *Inward Love and Compassion*
> g. *Surrender*
> h. *Commitment*

4. Step Four – Compassion (3 Minutes)

"May I Be Loving and Compassionate"

Practically speaking, love and compassion for others are the foundation stones for our own happiness and well-being. They are the universal currency of reciprocity between all beings, and the fundamental values that lie at the heart of all spiritual traditions. At this stage in our meditation process, we allow ourselves to be infused and immersed in the presence of universal love. We radiate love and compassion to all beings, including ourselves—love that spontaneously wishes happiness for all beings, and the compassion that constantly strives to remove the causes of their suffering. We vow to dedicate our lives to this loving and compassionate intention.

> a. *Exchange and Equalize Self and Others*
> b. *Interdependence and Universal Reciprocity*
> c. *Universal Essence*

5. Step Five – Mindfulness (5 Minutes)

"May I Be Focused and Mindful Through Breathing"

Calm, steady, and focused breathing are at the heart of many secular and spiritual techniques of meditation. When we breathe properly, we become less stressed and distracted; we are able to think more clearly, and to focus on the task at hand. Our blood-pressure drops, and our anxiety disappears. Many spiritual traditions teach deep and profound methods of breathing that balance our energies and center our consciousness deep within our being, where we are able to concentrate on our spiritual practice. In this step, we allow our consciousness to recede from our eyes, ears, nose, tongue, touch, thoughts, and emotions. As we breathe gently, our consciousness rides on the subtle breath into our heart center. This is the place that many traditions call 'the seat of the soul,' the core of our consciousness. Residing there, we may begin our own respective meditations, contemplations, and prayers. In this process, we learn to develop the capacity of 'mindfulness' and to observe our innermost thoughts, emotions, habits, and memories.

  a. Body Position
  b. Attention on the Breath
  c. Patience
  d. Inner Observation or Vigilance
  c. Recollection
  d. Concentration
  e. Observation

6. Step Six – Meditation (10 Minutes)

"May I Become Wise Through Meditation"

Now that the garden of our mind has been carefully cultivated, we can begin to deepen and expand the scope of our meditation. Honoring the profound and marvelous diversity among the world's contemplative traditions, we silently engage in the meditation of our own tradition or choosing, opening to transcendent insight, deep tranquility, or unity with that which is sacred to us. Mindful breathing itself can remain our sole focus or may provide a foundation for our chosen meditation. (See the various practices given below.)

  a. Tranquil Focus
  b. Insight
  c. Via Positiva and Via Negativa
  d. Bliss
  e. Equanimity
  f. Unity
  g. Absorption
  h. Transcendence

7. Step Seven – Dedication (3 Minutes)

"May I Serve All Beings
with Compassion, Peace, and Wisdom"

In order for our meditation to have power in our lives and benefit others, we must rededicate ourselves to our loving and compassionate intentions. May our meditation help us to engage in the world with wisdom and compassion. As we visualize our family, friends, enemies, colleagues, communities, and beings throughout the world, we vow to help alleviate their suffering and achieve sustainable love, peace and happiness for all.

In group practice, when the meditation is over and you emerge from silence together, you might find that your subsequent dialogue may reveal exhilarating new insights and bring you closer together. As Father Keating often says: "silence is the first language of the Divine, or that which we call God. Let us share in this silent communication before using words."

This meditation should be entered into with gentle compassion. At first, the discipline may be difficult, like starting a new exercise regime. But as with exercise, you may begin to see short-term results fairly quickly, though the more permanent, long-term changes will take time and perseverance. Like any other worthwhile life-venture, we need to be prepared to stick with the training and preparation required to fully reap the results. That is why it is so important to keep ourselves motivated. We should continually remind ourselves that these seven steps need to be practiced each day of our lives.

Finally, I strongly recommend that you keep a journal of your intentions for each of the seven steps. Each of these can yield profound inner guidance for all aspects of your life. There is an intimate and interdependent relationship between the quality of your daily life, your nighttime dreaming, and your meditations. Your journal will provide you with focal points for the actual meditation sessions and it will chart the progress of your contemplative journey through life.

GUIDELINES FOR INTERSPIRITUAL GROUP DISCUSSION & PRACTICE

Guidelines For InterSpiritual Group Discussion

The primary language of InterSpiritual dialog is silence. It is the soothing elixir that places each person and each tradition on neutral, reciprocal ground. In silence we are liberated from our fixed religious or non-religious identities and the words that distinguish one truth from another. We celebrate and welcome the diversity of our respective spiritual styles, traditions, racial, gender and ethnic diversity. Separately and jointly we experience a wordless quality or essence of being that unites us.

> When I am liberated by silence, when I am no longer involved in
> the measurement of life, but in the living of it, I can discover a
> form of prayer in which there is effectively no distraction.
> - Thomas Merton

When we enter into conversation with each other it is important that we maintain this same gentle and kind quality of being. Openness implies vulnerability. Therefore, we must take great care with our intentions and our words. Opening up to and with each other is rare and delicate occurrence. Therefore, we take great care not to cause another person's shy inner self to recede back into the shadows of his or her consciousness. We create a safe and supportive container within which this contemplative process can unfold.

Following are two sets of guidelines to aid us supporting one another. The first is a list that applies specifically to InterSpiritual dialogues. It is based on ten years of work with contemplative teachers from many traditions with the Spiritual Paths Foundation. The second comes from the work of Parker Palmer that he has termed, "Circles of Trust." Here he provides succinct "touchstones," as he calls them, to guide our conversations and our way of being with each other.

Guidelines Developed in Our Spiritual Paths Programs

- Embrace silence as a common language and the elixir of shared experience, expanding our exclusive identity to one that is more inclusive and universal.

- Genuinely celebrate and honor the diversity of all spiritual traditions.

- Soften the personal boundaries of fixed identity of our own religion and belief system and open our hearts for sincere sharing and learning from the experiences of others.

- We do not respond to a statement by another person by either disagreeing or agreeing. Instead, we simply listen compassionately, allowing the statement of another to rest in contemplative reflection and silence.

- Refrain from imposing or projecting our views on another's tradition, beliefs or practices.

- Refrain from imposing a single universal truth on all religions and spiritual traditions that might not be shared by the traditions themselves.

- If you belong to a specific tradition, speak from it as a participant rather than for it, as a sole representative.

- Be careful not to misappropriate, or lift out of context a specific practice from one tradition and graft it onto another tradition or your practice without knowing its indigenous meaning.

- Engage in contemplative, compassionate listening to draw out wisdom within each participant. Meditatively observe and release your inner judgments and impulse to react to their words.

Parker Palmer's Circles of Trust Touchstones

The following points were adapted from Parker Palmer's "Circles of Trust Touchstones." More information can be found in his book "A Hidden Wholeness," or at The Center for Courage and Renewal: www.couragerenewal.org. Palmer's methodology provides an extremely important grounding for InterSpiritual dialog.

- **Extend and receive welcome**. People learn best in hospitable spaces. In this circle, we support each other's learning by giving and receiving hospitality.

- **Be present as fully as possible**. Be here with your doubts, fears and failings as well as your convictions, joys, and successes, your listening as well as your speaking.

- **What is offered in the circle is by invitation, not demand**. This is not a "share or die" event! During this time, do whatever your soul calls for, and know that you do it with our support. Your soul knows your needs better than we do.

- **Speak your truth in ways that respect other people's truth**. Our views of reality may differ, but speaking one's truth in a circle of trust does not mean interpreting, correcting, or debating what others say. Speak from your center to the center of the circle, using "I" statements, trusting people to do their own sifting and winnowing.

- **No fixing, no saving, no advising, and no setting each other straight**. This is one of the hardest guidelines for those of us in the helping professions. But it is one of the most vital rules if we wish to make a space that welcomes soul, the inner teacher.

- **Learn to respond to others with honest, open questions instead of counsel, corrections**. With such questions, we help hear each other into deeper speech.

- **When the going gets rough, turn to wonder.** If you feel judgmental, or defensive, ask yourself, "I wonder what brought her to this belief?" or "I wonder what he's feeling right now?" or "I wonder what my reaction teaches me about myself?" Set aside judgment to listen to others—and to yourself—more deeply.

- **Attend to your own inner teacher**. We learn from others, of course. But as we explore poems, stories, questions, and silence in a circle of trust, we have a special opportunity to learn from within. So pay close attention to your own reactions and responses, to your most important teacher.

- **Trust and learn from the silence.** Silence is a gift in our noisy world, and a way of knowing in itself. Treat silence as a member of the group. After someone has spoken, take time to reflect without immediately filling the space with words.

- **Observe deep confidentiality**. Trust comes from knowing that group members honor confidences and take seriously the ethics of privacy and discretion.

- **Know that it's possible to leave the circle with whatever it was that you needed when you arrived**. Know that the seeds planted here can keep growing in the days ahead.

Acknowledgements

THERE ARE SO MANY PEOPLE who have been a part of this endeavor that I wish to thank. I will simply mention their names here without being specific as to why. Sadly, I will have forgotten some significant names that later editions will include. Please forgive me if yours is one of these. My deep gratitude to Reverend Gregg Anderson, Swami Atmarupananda, Reverend Lauren Atress, Rev. Diane Berke, John Bennett, Rabbi Ozer Bergman, Tessa Bielecki, Robert Bosnak, Harvey Bottelscn, Bikkhu Bodhi, Robert Bosnak, Joan Borysenko, Reverend Cynthia Bourgeault, Mary Ann Brussat, Loya Cespooch, Nancy Belle Coe, Sister Brahmaprana, Ken Cohen, Katherine and Roger Collis, Kathy Corcoran, Anita Daniel, Father Dave Denny, Laura Dixon, Geshe Lobsang Donyo, Lama Palden Drolma, Gordon Dveirin, Suzanne Farver, Mollie Favour, Rob Gabriel, Gelek Rinpoche, Stephanie Glatt, Dr. John Allen Grimes, Roshi Joan Halifax, George Haynes, Sheikh Kabir and Camille Helminski, Rabbi Brad Hirschfield, Sister Jose Hobday, James Hughes, Judy Hyde, Pir Zia Inayat-Khan, Edie Irons, Don "Four Arrows" Jacobs, Reverend Alan Jones, Chief Oren Lyons, Yogi Nataraja Kallio, Father Thomas Keating, Rabbi Miles Krassen, Dr. Michael Kearney, Reverend Master Khoten, Acharya Judy Lief, Rev. Aaron McEmrys, Robert McDermott, Dena Merriam, Netanel Miles-Yepez, Brad Miller, Sheikh Muhammad Jamal al-Jerrahi (Gregory Blann), Enrico and Nadia Natali, Rabbi Leah Novick, Carol Pearson, Susan Pierce, Lexie Potamkin, Reverend Tenzin Priyadarshi, Margot and Tom Pritzker, Lynda Rae, Imam Feisal Abdul Rauf, Jonathan and Diana Rose, Rabbi Jeff Roth, Sharon Salzburg, Barbara Sargent, Swami Sarvadevananda, Rabbi Zalman Schachter-Shalomi, Rabbi Arthur Gross Schaefer, Dr. Marilyn Schlitz, Christiane Schlumberger, Grace Alvarez Sesma, Rabbi Rami Shapiro, Acharya Judith Simmer-Brown, Ajahn Sona, Geshe Lhundup Sopa, Tina Staley, Michael Stranahan, Tekaronianeken Jake Swamp, Brother Wayne Teasdale, Geshe Lobsang Tenzin, Juliet Spahn-Twomey, Ani Tenzin Kacho, Pravrajika Vrajaprana, Dr. B. Alan Wallace, Radhule Weininger, Sharon Wells, Judy Whetstine, Catherine Wyler, and Paula Zurcher.

I am also grateful to all those who have studied InterSpiritual Meditation and the Spiritual Paths Mandala Process with me, for they have helped to clarify and refine the ideas and practices described herein. I am indebted to living examples of my mentors and teachers including Geshe Lhundup Sopa, Father Thomas Keating, Rabbi Zalman Schachter, and His Holiness the Dalai Lama. I also wish to thank Netanel Miles-Yepez for editing the book, Zachary Malone for preparing this workbook for publication, and Lynda Rae for the cover design. I am extremely grateful to Juliet Spohn Twomey, Stephanie Glatt and Kathy Corcoran and La Casa de Maria for providing encouragement and an incubator for this work. I am deeply grateful to the Aspen Chapel for providing the Aspen home for Spiritual Paths Foundation and our board of directors including Jay Hughes, Gregg Anderson, Suzanne Farver, John Bennett, Lexie Potamkin, Mike Stranahan and Harvey Bottlesen. And I am infinitely grateful to my family members, Alexandra and Nulty White, Jonathan Bastian, Paul Keeley, Marianne Bastian and to all my ancestors.